1986

The Principle of Double E

A Critical Appraisal of its Traditional Understanding

European University Studies

Europäische Hochschulschriften
Publications Universitaires Européennes

Series XXIII

Theology

Reihe XXIII   Série XXIII

Theologie
Théologie

Vol./Bd. 245

PETER LANG
Frankfurt am Main · Bern · New York

Lucius Iwejuru Ugorji

The Principle of Double Effect

A Critical Appraisal of its Traditional Understanding and its Modern Reinterpretation

PETER LANG

Frankfurt am Main · Bern · New York

CIP-Kurztitelaufnahme der Deutschen Bibliothek

Ugorji, Lucius Iwejuru:

The principle of double effect : a crit.
appraisal of its traditional understanding
and its modern reinterpretation / Lucius Iwejuru
Ugorji. - Frankfurt am Main ; Bern ; New York :
Lang, 1985.
  (European university studies : Ser. 23,
  Theology ; Vol. 245)
  ISBN 3-8204-5627-9
NE: Europäische Hochschulschriften / 23

Veröffentlicht mit Unterstützung des
Missionswissenschaftlichen Instituts MISSIO e.V.

ISSN 0721-3409
ISBN 3-8204-5627-9
© Verlag Peter Lang GmbH, Frankfurt am Main 1985

Printed by Weihert-Druck GmbH, Darmstadt

TABLE OF CONTENTS

PREFACE

Catholic moralists of the past repeatedly grappled with the problems posed by the moral norms commonly identified today as "deontological". In their endeavours to solve or at least mitigate these problems they employed the principle of double effect, a tool shrewdly designed by Catholic Tradition for this purpose. In reviewing some of these attempts John Lynch succintly remarked in 1956 that "while the principle of double effect endures, a moralist life need never be dull"(1).

The truth of this statement seems to be confirmed by the spate of literature that has emerged in recent times as lively and scholarly attempts at restudying the principle. Many of these modern studies have a new character. In contrast to the past, they are not concerned with the correct application of the principle to concrete cases nor are they interested in how it was understood by Tradition. They are, rather, mainly preoccupied with reformulating and reinterpreting it in a manner that makes it a fundemantal principle of a teleological ethics. Above and beyond, they level harsh criticisms on the traditional presentation of the principle in a tone that seems to suggest that Tradition has failed to understand the very rule it has itself formulated. A puzzling and intriguing assumption! This work, which was submitted to the University of Münster in the Winter Semester of 1983/ 84 as a dissertation for a doctorate degree in Sacred Theology, undertakes to attend to this paradox.

I wish to seize this space to express my deep sentiments of gratitude to all who stood by my side during the period of its production. In a very special way I owe immense gratitude to my teacher, Prof. Dr. Bruno Schüller SJ, for inspiring it and for accompanying me at each stage of my research with invaluable advice; to Dr. Dieter Witschen for his useful suggestions and to Dr. D. U. Mere for proofreading my manuscripts. I am also highly obliged to my diocese (Umuahia/Nigeria) for the generosity of granting me a study leave; to the proprietors of Missio Aachen for financing part of my research project; to my relations and friends for their kindness and solidarity.

Münster, 5. July 1984   Lucius I. Ugorji

---

1   John Lynch, "Notes on Moral Theology", ThSt, 17, (1956), 169-170.

INTRODUCTION

A) THE PROBLEM OF THE PRINCIPLE OF DOUBLE EFFECT AND PRESENT DAY RESEARCH

In his encyclical letter, **Humanae Vitae**, Pope Paul VI restates the traditional catholic doctrine on abortion (1), sterilization (2) and birth control (3) when he declares in article 14:

> We are obliged once more to declare that the direct inter-
> ruption of the generative process already begun and,
> above all direct abortion, even for therapeutic reasons,
> are absolutely excluded as lawful means of controlling the
> birth of children. Equally condemned ... is direct sterili-
> zation, whether of man or of the woman, whether perma-
> nent or temporary. Similarly excluded is any action, which
> either before, at the moment of, or after sexual inter-
> course, is specifically intended to prevent procreation,
> whether as an end or as a means."

The proclamation of these words dashed the hope of many who had anxiously looked foreward to a change or at least a modification of the traditional teaching on birth control. Far from being quietly received, this declaration provoked a great deal of discussions. Bishops' conferences (4) in various parts of the globe issued pastoral letters on the encyclical and strove to reconcile its doctrine as much as possible with the dilemmas of many married couples. Catholic scholars (5) on both sides of the Atlantic debated hotly over the

----

1   cf. Pius XI, Casti Connubii, AAS, 22(1930), pp. 562-564; John XXIII, Pacem in Terris, AAS, 55 (1963), pp. 259-260; Gaudium et Spes, n. 51.

2   cf. Pius XI, op. cit. AAS, 22(1930), p.565; Decres of the Holy Office, 22 Feb. 1940, AAS, 32(1940), p. 73; Pius XII, Address to Midwives, AAS 43(1951), pp. 843-844.

3   cf. Pius XI, op. cit., AAS, 22(1930), pp. 559-561; Pius XII, op. cit., AAS, 43(1951), p. 843; John XXIII, Matter et Magister, AAS, 52(1961), p. 447.

4   cf. Eduardus Hamel, "Conferentiae Episcopales et Encylclica "Hu-
    manae Vitae". Periodica, 58(1969), 234-349; John Horgan ed.; **Hu-
    manae Vitae and the Bishops.** The Encyclical and the Statements of the National Hierarchies, (Ireland 1972).

5   cf. John L. Russel, "Contraception and the Natural Law". Heythrop Journal, 10(1969), 121-134; George M. Regan, "Natural Law in the Church Today", **Catholic Lawyer**, 13(1967), 21-41; Joseph Fuchs, S.J. **Natural Law - A Theological Investigation** (New York 1965); F. Henrich ed., **Naturgesetz und christliche Ethik.** Zur wissenschaft-
    lichen Diskussion nach Humanae Vitae (München 1970).

encyclical and set themselves the added task of some critical study of the traditional teaching on the Natural Law on which this doctrine was erected.

As these debates progressed the issues discussed widened. Related questions like homologous artificial insemination, masturbation, transplantation of organs, premarital sexual relations and the like attracted critical attention. The normative propositions proscribing these acts are justified by Catholic Tradition in a manner fundamentally the same. They are said to be intrinsic (moral) evils which are prohibited under every circumstance apart from any consideration of their consequences and the intention of the agent.

The validity of this way and manner of grounding ethical norms is being greeted with much sceptical reserve by many contemporary catholic moralists. They ask whether any conceivable act could be morally evaluated in isolation from the effects it produces. At the centre of their discussions over this issue is the classical principle of double effect which governs a good and an intrinsic (moral) evil producing act.

Some of the acts, like the killing of an innocent person, governed by this principle are usually normed deontologically by catholic tradition. Ample evidence shows that a strict application of the deontological norms leads to conclusions that appear to contradict moral common sense. An example which is often chosen to illustrate this point is the rare case of ectopic gestation where an embryo is developing in the fallopian tube. If the embryo is left to develop in the tube, the tube will certainly rupture and consequently both mother and child will die. When doctors established that the tube itself is pathological, catholic moralists applied the principle of double effect to the case and deemed it permitted for doctors to excise the tube with the intention of curing the pathology. They realized that the procedure will save the life of the mother while the non-viable foetus will perish with the excised tube. The restoration of the woman's health is considered the good effect intended; the death of the child is deemed a non-intended side-effect.

The same moralists deem it forbidden for surgeons to shell out the embryo from the tube - a procedure which heals the pathology while leaving the tube and the woman's fecundity intact. Doing this, they say, is equivalent to a directly intended killing of an innocent person. To intend such an act directly even as a means to a proportionate good, they maintain, is always morally reprehensible.

A strict application of the deontological norm prohibiting the killing of an innocent person would result in both mother and child perishing. By applying the principle of double effect to this case catholic tradition narrows down the area where the deontological prohibition of killing is strictly binding and so is able to save the life of the mother at least. Nevertheless, catholic tradition, in deeming the shelling out of the foetus from the tube forbidden, by its application of the principle of double effect, appears to prohibit a course of action that does lesser harm to the woman and permits the alternative whereby the woman loses both her fallopian tube and fertility.

12

If one recalls that when one is faced with the options of choosing between different courses of action that cause harm, the preference rule requires that one chooses that alternative that causes the least harm, it then looks like the principle of double effect commands an apparently morally wrong act by prescribing the alternative that causes more harm. This paradoxical state of affairs attracts a lot of name-callings and scornful remarks towards catholic moral theology. This tradition is, for instance, said to be guilty of subtle quibbling and blind hairsplitting (6) and legalism. In the latter regard Joseph Fletcher (7) scoffs at the catholic tradition in these words:

> "With Catholics it has taken the form of a fairly ingenuous moral theology that, as its twists and involutions have increased, resorts more and more to a causistry that appears (as, to its credit, it does) to evade the very "laws" of right and wrong laid down in its textbooks and manuals."

Many modern catholic moralists in trying, as it were, to show some moral common sense in their evaluation of the case of ectopic gestation, described above, maintain that the shelling out of the embryo is morally preferable on grounds that it causes lesser damage than the alternative of excising the tube (8). Therefore for reasons of consistency they find a restudy of the principle of double effect, which in this case proscribes the more desirable course of action, an urgent task.

The restudy centres mainly on the function and moral relevance of the principle. In reply to the question about the function of the principle Peter Knauer (9) asserts that "rightly understood" the rule of double effect functions as the fundamental principle of normative ethics which specifies when the permission or causation of a physical evil is justified and when it is not. Bruno Schüller (10) and Franz Scholz (11) indicate that the principle serves tradition the purpose of a restrictive interpretation of deontological norms.

----

6   cf. W. van der Marck, **Love and Fertility.** Contemporary Questions about Birth Regulation, trans. C. A.L. Jarrott, (New York 1965), p. 51.

7   Joseph Fletcher, **Situation Ethics.** The New Morality, (London 1966), p. 19.

8   Peter Knauer, "Das rechtverstandene Prinzip der Doppelwirkung als Grundnorm jeder Gewissensentscheidung", in: ThGl, 57(1967), 124; Charles Curran, "Absolute Norms and Medical Ethics", in: ibid. ed. **Absolutes in Moral Theology?** Washington D.C. 1968, pp. 112 ff.

9   Peter Knauer, art. cit., pp. 111-112.

10 Bruno Schüller, **Die Begründung sittlicher Urteile.** Typen ethischer Argumentation in der Moraltheologie, Düsseldorf 1980, pp. 133-141.

11 Franz Scholz, **Wege, Umwege und Auswege aus der Moraltheologie,** (München 1976), pp. 40 ff.

The question regarding the moral relevance of the principle rotates mainly around the moral significance of the direct/indirect distinction of the rule. In this regard different questions are posed.
First, it is asked whether there is a difference between an intending
and a permitting will. In reply to this question Schüller (12) says
yes, if this distinction is applied to a moral evil. On the other hand,
he replies with a "no" to this question, if this distinction is applied
to a non-moral evil. This, he says, can be intended as a means to
a proportionate good. Richard McCormick (13) challenges this view. To
his mind, if there is a difference between both in the face of a moral
evil, this difference must also be obtainable when a non-moral evil
is considered. However, with the appearance of "The Double Effect in
Catholic Thought: a Reevalution", an article in which Schüller (14)
argues his point further, McCormick (15) withdraws his objection.

Second, it is also inquired whether the direct/indirect distinction
plays a morally decisive role. That this distinction plays a morally
significant role in the realm of acts teleologically normed is not a
matter of controversy. What is controverted is the moral decisive
nature of its application to deontological norms. In his contribution
to the debate Albert Di Ianni (16) argues that the distinction always
plays a morally significant role.

In contrast, an overriding number of eminent catholic moralists
are of the opinion that this distinction is merely descriptive when
applied to deontological norms. However, the argumentative strategies
they employ in reaching this conclusion are different. At least two
genres of these strategies are discernable.

The first consists in the approach of some moralists who attend
to this question by trying to show that the condition of the principle

----

12 Bruno Schüller, "Direct Killing/Indirect Killing", in: Charles Curran and Richard McCormick eds., **Readings in Moral Theology No.
1: Moral Norms and Catholic Tradition**, (New York 1979), pp. 139-
140. This article appeared first as "Direkte/indirekte Tötung", in:
ThPh., 47(1972), pp. 341-357.

13 Richard McCormick, "Ambiguity in Moral Choice", in: ibid. and
Paul Ramsey, **Doing Evil to Achieve Good**, (Chicago 1978), pp. 30-
31.

14 Bruno Schüller, "The Double Effect in Catholic Thought: a Reevaluation", in: Richard McCormick and Paul Ramsey, ed. op. cit., pp.
168-192.

15 Richard McCormick, "A Commentary on the Commentaries", in: ibid.
pp. 263 ff.

16 Albert Di Ianni, "The Direct/Indirect Distinction in Morals", in:
Thomist, 41(1977), pp. 350-380. McCormick criticizes Di Ianni's
argument as question begging. Cf. McCormick, **Notes on Moral Theology 1965 Through 1981**, (Washington 1981), pp. 713-723.

which requires that the good effect should proceed from the act at least, as immediately and directly as the evil is an instance of "physicalism". These moralists conclude from this that the direct/indirect distinction founded on purely physical categories cannot be rightly considered as having any moral significance.

The second consists in the approach of Scholz (17) who believes that the above condition of the principle is not concretely realizable, because, as he sees it, an action can have only one natural (per se) effect. If this natural effect is evil, he maintains that it is willed as a means to the good end. Thus in such a case the direct/indirect distinction can no longer be the question.

Although these moralists may differ in their argumentative strategies, they all agree that only the condition requiring a proportionate reason is morally functional here. By down-playing or dismissing the moral relevance of the traditional direct/indirect distinction, while upholding "proportionate reason" as the only morally decisive element in the moral appraisal of deontological norms, these modern moralists try to justify the moral rightness or wrongness of acts governed by these norms along teleological reasoning. This represents, in its own way, the increasing inclination of many contemporary catholic moralists towards adopting teleological argumentations in justifying ethical norms.

B) THE AIM AND SCOPE OF THIS WORK

This work undertakes to state and critically appraise the traditional presentation and application of the principle of double effect with the view to determining the extent its reformulation or reinterpretation by some modern moralists is justifiable. Its first part delimits and examines the areas where the principle is traditionally applied in order to establish the role played by the direct/indirect distinction which forms the core of the rule. Its second part devotes attention towards examining the modern reinterpretation of the principle. It is not possible to present and critically appraise each of the modern attempts at reinterpreting the principle. Trying to do this will not only be futile but also will be fruitless. At best it would consist in a superficial presentation of different opinions. At worst it will consist in a work so densely packed with divergent views which leaves a reader none the wiser.

To obviate both extremes the works of two German authors, Knauer and Scholz, have been chosen. This choice has been made for two reasons. First, both authors reflect faithfully the general tendency of

---

17 Franz Scholz, op. cit., pp. 81 ff.; see also N. Hendriks, **Le moyen mauvais pour obtenir une fin bonne.** Essai sur la troisième condition du principe de L'acte à double effet, Roma 1981.

many catholic moralists towards dissolving the principle of double effect into a teleological rule. Second, both authors differ considerably in the way and manner they set out to achieve this objective. Unlike Scholz, Knauer represents the group of moralists that bring a charge of "physicalism" against the catholic tradition. In contrast to Knauer, Scholz represents the group of moralists that argue that a "causa per se" cannot produce two "per se" effects simulteneously. Unlike Scholz, Knauer reinterpretes certain key terms of the principle.

One who occupies himself with reading the spate of literature that has been published in recent times on the principle of double effect can scarcely fail to detect the ambiguity in the use of terms that has pervaded the discussion. Joseph A. Selling (18) comments on the undesirable result proceeding from such equivocal use of terms when he says:

> "A great deal of what is being written today concerns the meanings of terms which have their origin in the application of this principle. The meanings of direct/indirect, intended/unintended, willing/permitting have come under scrutiny and have been analyzed so much that it has become hard to determine what one should think of them. To make matters more difficult, there are seemingly endless permutations possible when we combine these terms not only with themselves but with the other relevant categories of act/effect, good/evil, moral/premoral."

Such equivocal use of terms leads to confusion and nothing else. This work also intends to dispel this confusion. Thus a close attention will be paid to clarification of the key technical terms employed in the formulation of the principle. The meaning of these terms will be established not only by consulting their text book definitions but also by examining their concrete illustrations.

C) CLARIFICATION OF TERMS

Some technical terms frequently employed in the present day discussions of the principle of double effect include descriptive and pre-

---

18 Joseph A. Selling, "The Problem of Reinterpreting the Principle of Double Effect", in: Louvain Studies, VIII(1981), p.50.

scriptive language (19), moral goodness and moral rightness (20), teleology and deontology. No doubt, many contemporary moralists are familiar with these terms. But since it is not seldom that scholars employ the same words but mean different things it might be worthwhile at the very beginning to clarify the senses in which these words will be used in this work in order to preclude every ambiguity.

1) DESCRIPTIVE AND PRESCRIPTIVE LANGUAGE

It may happen that in talking about a person "X" one makes the following statements:

A) X is known in this city.

B) X is famous in this city.

C) X is notorious in this city.

Although all these propositions speak of the knowledge of "X", they do not mean exactly the same. The semantic contents of Propositions B and C are greater than those of A; they incorporate proposition A in their semantic comprehension. Above and beyond, both (B and C) give the sense in which "X" is known. While the knowledge of "X" in proposition B is in a positive or good sense, it is negative in proposition C. Similarly it may happen that in speaking of the alteration in a situation "X" one asserts that:

A) X is changing.

B) X is progressing.

C) X is undergoing a decadence.

Proposition "A" simply **describes** the situation "X" without indicating whether the alteration that has occurred is good or bad. Apart from indicating that some alternations have occurred propositions "B" and "C" also show that these changes are good (positive) and bad (negative) respectively.

Words like "change" and "known" in proposition A in each of the above examples are usually called **descriptive terms**. Some illustrations of these terms within the realm of moral philosophy and theology would include: killing a human being, removal of others' property,

----

19 v. Rudolf Ginters, **Werte und Normen**. Einführung in die philosophische und theologische Ethik (Düsseldorf 1982), pp. 42-44; L. Janssens, "Norms and Priorities in a love Ethics", in: Louvain Studies 6(1977), pp. 207-238; R.M. Hare, **The Language of Morals** (New York 1982), pp. 1-17, 111-126.

20 cf. Bruno Schüller, **Die Begründung sittlicher Urteile**, pp. 133-141.

making a false statement, eating, drinking, following a command, having sexual relationship outside wedlock, the use of artificial contraceptive devices, artificial insemination and so on.

Words like progressing, decadence, famous and notorious, in propositions B and C in each of the above examples are said to be **prescriptive (normative or evaluative) terms**. Some prescriptive terms designate non-moral values or non-moral disvalues (21) like killing an innocent person, killing an injust aggressor. Others refer to moral values or moral disvalues. Good illustrations of these from the hand books of moral theology would be: murder, adultery, rape, lying, gluttony, patience, obedience, stealing, robbery, humility, patience, chastitiy, scandal, and so on.

Judging from the type of language employed in illustrating intrinsic (moral) evils in the hand books of moral theology various classes of such evils are discernable. Some are presented in moral prescriptive or value terms like: lying, murder, blasphemy and the like. The introduction of such value-terms into normative statements give rise **to analytic judgements** whose truth-values depend solely on the meaning of the words employed. Such judgments or propositions tell a listener or reader, who comprehends the meanings of the words employed in them, nothing new and so are communicatively empty. Thus statements like "stealing is always morally prohibited", "thou shall never commit murder not even as a means of saving the lives of one thousand persons", "leading others into sin is always morally reprehensible", "cooperating in the sin of another is morally wrong" are at best tautological and pose no problems in moral discourses, if only the disputants understand the meaning of the value-terms employed.

Other illustrations of intrinsic (moral) evils, in the hand books of moral theology are rendered in non-moral prescriptive terms like the killing of an innocent person. Still other illustrations are given in purely descriptive terms like: the use of artificial contraceptive devices, artificial insemination and so on. The introduction of these terms into normative statements give rise to **synthetic judgments**. In contrast to moral prescriptive terms when non-moral prescriptive terms or purely descriptive terms are used in making normative statements their truth values are not self-evident. Accordingly one who employs them in a normative proposition is obliged to back them with some logical reasons. Depending on how compelling the reasons adduced are, difference of opinion may arise between a listener (reader) and a speaker (author) and thus a moral controversy is born.

---

21 For the distinction between moral and non-moral value and disvalue cf. B. Schüller, ibid. pp. 73-79; W. Wolbert, **Ethische Argumentation und Paränese in 1 Kor 7**, Düsseldorf 1981, pp. 30-33; W. Frankena, **Ethics**, New York 1963, pp. 47-48.

2) MORAL GOODNESS AND MORAL RIGHTNESS

Paul in his letter to the Romans describes moral goodness when he says:

> "Avoid getting into debt, except the debt of mutual love. If you love your fellow men you have carried out your obligations. All the commandments: ... are summed up in this single command. You must love your neighbours as yourself. Love is one thing that cannot hurt your neighbour" (Rom 13, 8-10).

The person who acts out of the disposition of benevolence or love behaves in a **morally good** manner. Since he acts out of an impartial love he cannot but choose the course of action he sincerely believes will further the welfare of his neighbour. Of course, it may happen that in doing that which he believes would advance the welfare of his neighbour he may, by some miscalculations, end up harming him instead. To this extent his act is **morally wrong**.

In contrast to acting out of a disposition of benevolence, a person may be motivated solely by purely egoistic or self-seeking designs. By acting out of such a motive he performs a **morally bad** act. Of course it may be the case that he contributes to the welfare of his fellow men. In this respect he performs a **morally right** act. This distinction between moral badness and moral rightness is discernable in Paul's teaching on work-righteousness (22). The work-righteous man is "ex definitione" morally bad. Nevertheless, he could do the morally right by fasting, giving of alms and praying regularly. This distinction between moral goodness and moral rightness is also reflected in Kant's well known distinction between acting from a sense of duty (aus Pflicht) and preforming what is somebody's duty (pflichtgemäß) (23).

Combining the different moral characters of the dispositions of an agent with the different moral characters of the acts he could perform vis a vis the welfare of his fellow men, four computations are possible. The acts my be either:

a) morally good and morally right; or

b) morally good and morally wrong; or

c) morally bad and morally right; or

d) morally bad and morally wrong.

----

22 Bruno Schüller, **Gesetz und Freiheit.** Eine moral-theologische Untersuchung, Düsseldorf 1966, pp. 150-151.

23 Immanuel Kant, Groundwork of the **Metaphysic of Morals,** tr. H.J. Paton, New York, 3. Aufl., 1964, pp.64 ff.

The principle of double effect is concerned with specifying the conditions under which the act it governs may be said to be morally right or morally wrong. Thus the present day discussions on the principle concerns or should concern the moral rightness and moral wrongness of the acts to which the rule applies.

3) TELEOLOGY AND DEONTOLOGY

The diverse opinions propounded by moralists on how the moral rightness and wrongness of acts are to be established naturally invite classification. One of such classifications is offered by dichotomies popular for their promise to organize a multitude of disagreements around a fundamental one from which they are derived. One dichotomy that has become well known among moral philosophers and theologians in recent times is the distinction between teleology and deontology (24) introduced by C.D. Broad (25) in 1930 as an apparent improvement on Sidgwick's trichotomy (intuitionism, egoism and utilitarianism).

According to Broad (26) teleological theories assert that the moral rightness or wrongness of an act is "always determined by its tendencies to produce certain consequences which are intrinsically good or bad", while deontological theories claim that "such and such a kind of action would always be right (or wrong) in such and such circumstances, no matter what its consequences might be". Evidently this disjunction is neat and logically elegant. Nevertheless, this logical elegance is bought at a great price (27). Moralists who differ from one another are brought under the same umbrella on account of this neat disjunction. A few examples will help to highlight some irreconcilable differences existing in the teachings of various moralists yoked together by Broad's division.

Teleologists generally agree that it is their task to provide guidelines for the good or even the best possible life for man. They agree further that this can be done by finding answers to two fundamental

----

24 Teleology and deontology are etymologically taken from the Greek **telos** and **deon** respectively. The former means "end" and the latter "duty".

25 cf. C.D. Broad, **Five Types of Ethical Theories**, London 1 ed., 1930, 2 ed. 1979; F. Paulsen, **System der Ethik** (Berlin 1 ed. 1889, 10 ed. 1913), pp. 221, distinguishes between formal and deontological theories; B. Schüller introduced the distinction between teleology and deontology in the catholic moral tradition in his "**Die Begründung sittlicher Urteile**", (Düsseldorf 1 ed. 1973, 2 ed. 1980).

26 C.D. Broad, op. cit. p. 206.

27 cf. B. Schüller, "The Double Effect in Catholic Thought: a Reevaluation", in: Richard McCormick and Paul Ramsey (eds.), **Doing Evil to Achieve Good**, Chicago 1978, p. 167.

ethical questions: What is good and what is to be done? However, they begin to part company with one another in replying to questions like: 1) What is good? 2) Whose good is to be taken into account? To the first question a variety of answers are offered. There are monistic answers that maintain that there is only one good, for instance happiness, pleasure, satisfaction of desire, self-realization or perfection, power or knowledge (28). There are also pluralistic answers which include all or most of the goods outlined by monists.

Regarding the question on whose good is to be promoted, Ethical egoism as propounded by Epicurus, Hobbes, and Nietzsche maintains that a man is always to do what will promote his greatest good. Thus an act or a rule of action is right if and only if it promotes a balance of good or evil for an agent in the long run as any alternative would. In contrast, Ethical universalism or what is often referred to as utilitarianism insists that the greatest good of all concerned should be taken into account. Thus an act or a rule of action is right if and only if it probably can produce as great a balance of good over evil in the world as a whole as any other alternative would (29).

Generally, deontological theories argue that the morality of certain acts are not determined exclusively from their consequences. Nevertheless, they propound different opinions as to whether or not ethical norms are to be considered always absolutely binding without exception (30). Intuitionists like, W.D. Ross, consider a moral prohibition against falsehood a 'prima facie' duty (duty all things considered). Kant, Fichte and Catholic tradition deem it absolutely binding. Reflecting over the sharp differences existing in the ethical theories generally considered deontological by contemporary moralists, Schüller (31) remarks:

"Only Kant, Fichte and the Catholic tradition assert that there are actions that are morally wrong without any regard for their consequences. W.D. Ross and the modern critics of utilitarianism, on the contrary, assert that for the moral rightness of an action consequences always play a determining role, but not alone ... In this light, only Kant and the Catholic tradition, but not the modern critics

----

28 William Frankena, **Ethics**, New York 1963, p. 15.

29 ibid, pp. 15-16.

30 Here it is helpful to call to mind the two senses in which ethical norms could be understood, namely as "lex indita" (pneuma) and as "lex scripta" (gramma). **Lex indita** binds absolutely. **Lex scripta** admits of exceptions in so far as it is difficult to cloth the sense of a norm or law in human language. See also Schüller, "Neuere Beiträge zum Thema Begründung sittlicher Normen", Theologische Berichte 4, Einsiedeln: Benziger 1974, pp. 114-115.

31 Bruno Schüller, ibid. p. 177.

of utilitarianism, know deontological norms as defined by
C.D. Broad."

Apart from grouping ethical theories radically different from one
another under one banner, Broad's clear-cut division seems to have
one other serious weakness; it appears to identify deontological theories with absolutism. By so doing, it excludes from the company of
deontologists a group of philosophers, for instance, the Oxford Intuitionists W.D. Ross, E. F. Carritt, who are often treated as deontologists "par excellence" and who reject absolutism as well as forms of
consequentialism.

These weaknesses call for some modifications in Broad's classification. One of such modifications is made by Richard A. McCormick (32).
He could be seen as placing moralists of diverse ethical theories on
a scale. At one end of the scale are absolute deontologists, whom he
identifies as Kant, Catholic tradition, Grisez, and Anscombe. At the
other end of the scale are absolute consequentialists among whom he
numbers Joseph Fletcher and some utilitarians. Moderate teleologists
take the golden mean and these are Ross, McCloskey, Frankena,
Fuchs, Knauer, Schüller, Böckle, Curran an so on.

It is not easy to detect what "principium divisionis" McCormick
employs in grouping these moralists in their various classes. However,
it is easy to note one shortcoming in his classification. This consists
in the fact that moralists like Ross, McCloskey and Frankena whom
McCormick groups under moderate teleologists are classically considered deontologists.

In a slightly different way Schüller enumerates three general
approaches, one teleological and two deontological. Teleological
(utilitarian, consequentists), theories are said to assert that the moral rightness of any action is exclusively determined by its consequences. Such theories maintain that ultimately one principle, namely,
the principle of benevolence, determines what is right and wrong.
Thus any tradition that understands benevolence as love (agape) is
classifiably under the teleological theory.

Deontological theories are to be understood as holding that at
least there are certain actions morally appraised not solely by their
consequences. At least two types of such theories are distinguishable.
The first type holds that the moral rightness of any action is determined always also, but not always solely, by its consequences.
Deontological theories of this sort are said to assume that there are

---

32 McCormick, "Reflections on the Literature", McCormick and C. Curran ed., **Moral Theology No. 1**, New York 1980, p. 318.

33 B. Schüller, Begründung, 1980, p. 282 ff.

two (34) or three (35) or even more (36) moral principles in no way reducible to one single principle. The second type of deontological theories maintains that there are at least some actions whose moral quality is completely independent of their consequences. Schüller observes that this type of deontological theory is propounded by the Catholic moral tradition.

Although McCormick groups the ethical methodologies of Ross, McCloskey and Frankena under teleological theories while Schüller classifies them under deontological, both agree that the sort of deontological theory propounded in Catholic tradition is of the strict type. When Catholic tradition is described as sponsoring a deontological ethical methodology, it should be understood in this strict sense.

---

34 W.K. Frankena, op. cit., p. 35-42, enumerates love and justice.

35 D. Lyons, **Form and Limits of Utilitarianism**, Oxford 1970, maintains that there are three principles: Love, Justice and fairness.

36 W.D. Ross, op. cit., p. 21, enumerates the following principles: duties of fidelity, reparation, gratitude, justice, benevolence, self improvement, not injuring others, while N.J. McCloskey, **Meta-Ethics and Normative Ethics**, The Hague 1969, pp. 223-241, counts four of such principles: promoting the good and removing of evil, justice, respect of persons and honesty.

PART ONE

THE TRADITIONAL UNDERSTANDING OF THE PRINCIPLE

1.

THE PRINCIPLE OF DOUBLE EFFECT:
ITS TRADITIONAL APPLICATION, FORMULATION
AND HISTORICAL BACKGROUND

In performing each voluntary act a man sets out to achieve a good or a value. While he attains some goods by means of elicited acts of the will, others are achieved by means of commanded acts. In the latter case the will goes outside itself, as it were, to achieve its object and in doing so its internal activity becomes as complicated as the world of external things. It seeks objects as they exist in reality outside itself and chooses or rejects them with their individual modifications including those of cause and effect. A man may, for instance, desire to calm his nerves and forget his sorrows. To attain this end he may choose a means that causes more than he intends. He may, for instance, choose to take alcohol which has a calming effect as well as the unintended side effect of reducing the reliability of his reaction in traffic. Similarly, an owner of a factory may sincerely desire to expedite the rate of production of goods in his enterprise. To attain this objective he may choose, as means, the introduction of heavy machines which, in addition, have the undesired side-effect of polluting the enviroment. Both the ends and means as well as the side-effects are willed but they are willed in different ways.

Catholic textbooks of moral theology describe the willing of the end and the means as **direct voluntary** (voluntarium directum or voluntarium in se). The willing of the end is termed "voluntarium in se et propter se", while the willing of the means is said to be "voluntarium in se sed non propter se". The willing of the side-effect is known as **indirect voluntary** (voluntarium indirectum or voluntarium in causa). The object of indirect voluntary is merely tolerated or permitted as the unavoidable side-effect of that which is directly willed.

This distinction between direct and indirect voluntariness is employed by handbooks of moral theology in the moral evaluation of certain acts that produce some good as well as some intrinsic (moral) evil. This distinction is usually made, for instance, in the moral assessment of an act by which an evil is avoidable or a good attainable only when disvalues like the killing of an innocent person, sterilization, self-pollution, artificial contraception, scandal, cooperation in the sin of others are produced. Any of these acts is qualified as "direct" if the person performing it intends it in so far as it is productive of any of these intrinsic (moral) evils, or as it is traditionally stated when the person intends the evil effect. Such is the case, for instance, when the sole immediate effect of an act is the so called intrinsic (moral) evil, namely, when the good effect is produced through the intrinsic (moral) evil. In this case the evil effect is necessarily intended as a means of attaining the good effect. In contrast, any of these acts is qualified as "indirect" if it is not intended in so far as it is productive of an intrinsic (moral) evil or as it is traditionally put, if the evil effect is not intended but merely tolerated. It is the case, for instance, when the intrinsic (moral) evil follows from the good effect or when it proceeds as immediately from the act as the good effect.

The importance attached to the direct/indirect distinction is evident from the role it places in the moral assessment of these acts which simultaneously produce a value and an intrinsic (moral) evil. When these acts are described as "direct" they are absolutely prohibited. Thus direct scandal, direct (formal) cooperation, direct killing of an innocent person and the like are judged morally wrong independent of their consequences and irrespective of the good intentions of the person performing them (1). On the other hand, when these acts are qualified as indirect their consequences are taken into account in their moral evaluation. In this case they may be permitted for a proportionate reason. Thus indirect scandal, indirect (material) cooperation, and the indirect killing of an innocent person are permitted when the prescriptions of the principle of double effect are satisfied.

1.1. A CONCRETE APPLICATION OF THE PRINCIPLE

A classical application of the principle of double effect is illustrated by the rare case of operating on a pregnant woman with a diseased uterus. If the surgical operation is omitted the cancer will spread. Both mother and child will die as a result. If, on the other hand, a hysterectomy is performed, the mother will be saved, while the child dies. The performance of this operation in this case where the death of the child is foreseen to result is justifiable by applying the principle of double effect. The act, which is seen as the cutting of the uterus, is said to be indifferent, that is to say, morally neutral. Only the good effect – the health of the mother – is intended; the evil effect – the death of the foetus – is not intended but merely permitted as an unavoidable side effect of that which is directly intended. Both the health of the mother (good effect) and the death

----

1 A few citations from the manuals will help to show how strictly direct killing of the innocent is prohibited. A. Lehmkuhl, **Theologia moralis**, Freiburg 1914, nr. 1000: "To directly kill an innocent person is always a most serious offence"; D. Prümmer, **Manuale Theologiae Moralis**, Vol. 2, Freiburg 12 ed. 1955, nr. 134: "Craniotomy and other surgical operations which directly bring about the death of the fetus are entirely forbidden." Noldin Schmitt, **Summa Theologiae moralis**, Vol. 2, 20 ed. 1930, no. 343, 4: "Abortion is then also forbidden if the mother is in certain danger of death and there is no other means of saving her". B. Häring, **Das Gesetz Christi**, Vol. III, Freiburg 1961, pp. 261 f.: "The church maintains inexorably the principle that it is under no circumstances permitted to attack directly the life of an innocent child in the womb."

of the child (evil effect) proceed with equal immediacy from the cutting of the uterus (indifferent act). The life of the mother is a value high enough to warrant sacrificing the life of the child by an indirect intention.

It is remarkable to note that the woman's health could also be restored by shelling out the foetus from the uterus – a less harmful procedure which above all preserves the woman's fertility. This procedure, which is judged immoral, is a violation of the principle of double effect because the health of the woman is achieved as a result of fetal death (2). In this case the destruction of the fetus will be directly intended as a means to restoring the woman's health.

1.2. THE FORMULATION OF THE PRINCIPLE OF DOUBLE EFFECT IN TRADITIONAL MANUALS

The principle of double effect, which seems to be exclusively used in the catholic tradition, has various formulations. In some handbooks it consists of four conditions. In other textbooks it is stated in three or two conditions. Still in others it is expressed in one compound statement. The verbal differences evident in the diverse formulations of the principle does not affect its substance; in its various presentations the principle remains substantially the same. A comparative glance at four classical formulations of the principle will prove helpful in driving home this point.

1) Benedictus Henricus Merkelbach O.P. (3) states the principle as follows: It is licit to posit a cause which produces a good and evil effect simultaneously, if the good effect follows from the cause as immediately as the evil or is not mediated by the evil and there is a proportionate grave reason which are always necessary, namely, that the action is "in se" licit and the agent has a good intention.

2) Joseph Mausbach and Gustav Ermecke (4) formulate the principle in the following way: One may perform or omit an act, although one foresees its evil consequence and could have prevented it, when the following four conditions exist:

a) The cause, the act, ought to be good in itself or at least indifferent. If it is bad, then it is always forbidden as sinful.

b) The good effect should proceed from the cause as immediately as the evil effect. If the evil effect proceeds first and the good effect follows from it, the act will be forbidden, since a good end does not sanctifiy an evil means.

----

2 cf. ibid. p. 226.

3 Benedictus Henricus Merkelbach, **Summa Theologiae Moralis**, Vol. 1, (Brugis Belgia 1956), p. 258.

4 Joseph Mausbach and Gustav Ermecke, **Katholische Moraltheologie**, Vol. 1, Münster 8 ed. 1954, p. 258.

c) The end, the intention of the agent, ought to be morally good. The evil effect should not be directly intended but merely permitted.

d) There ought to be a correspondingly grave reason, for instance, a positive, personal or general value or welfare, which outweighs the negative evil consequence.

3) Gerald Kelly (5) presents the rule in this manner: It is licit to perform an action which has good and bad effects provided.

a) that the action itself is not morally bad;

b) that the evil effect is sincerely not desired, but merely tolerated;

c) that the evil is not the means of obtaining the good effect; and

d) that the good effect is sufficiently important to balance or outweigh the harmful effect.

4) E.F. Regatillo and M. Zalba (6) word the principle as follows:

It is lawful to posit a cause or omit an action from which two effects follow, one good, the other evil, provided that:

a) the cause itself is good or indifferent;

b) only the good effect is approved of and intended; the evil effect may neither be willed nor wished;

c) the good effect should at least be equally immediate as the evil effect, in the sense that it is not obtained by means of the evil, lest the evil effect will be really intended "in se" as a means, as for instance, telling a lie in order to save a life;

d) there is a proportionate reason for positing the cause on account of the good effect proceeding from it, so that all things considered the cause of acting is evidently reasonable, as for instance, injuring an unjust aggressor in order so save one's life.

1.2.1. APPRECIATION OF THE PRESCRIPTIONS OF THE PRINCIPLE

The above formulations of the principle, though differently phrased, are in essence the same. Firstly, they all assert that an act which produces evil, as well as, good results could be performed under certain circumstances. Though none of the formulations expressly states whether the evil in question is "malum physicum" or "malum morale", the example of "lying" used by Regatillo and Zalba as illustration of an evil suggests that the type of evil under reference may be taken to be "malum morale".

----

5 Gerald Kelly, **Medico-Moral Problems**, St. Louis 1949, p. 12.

6 E.F. Regatillo and M. Zalba, **Theologiea Moralis Summa**, Vol. 1, Matriti 1952, p. 211.

Secondly, apart from Kelly, they all state that the act in itself should be good or at least indifferent. Kelly expresses the same idea negatively by asserting that the act in itself should not be morally wrong. Were the object (finis operis) of the act to be an intrinsic (moral) evil, it can never be used as a licit means to obtaining semen for the purpose of artificial insemination.

Thirdly, all the four formulations require that the intention of the agent be good, that is to say, only the good effect may be directly intended; the evil effect has to be indirectly intended. This condition reflects the scholastic dictum: "voluntas volendo malum fit mala", a dictum which is meaningful only if the evil in question is a moral evil, since a non moral evil is licitly intended as a "bonum utile". It is possible to will evil as an apparent good either "propter se" as an end or "in se sed non propter se" as a means. If the structure of the act performed is such that the good effect is achieved through the evil, then in willing the good effect, one wills the evil effect "in se sed non propter se". Thus, in acquiring sperm for the purpose of artificial insemination by means of masturbation, one necessarily intends this (intrinsic) evil means and accordingly the act is said to proceed out of a bad intention.

Fourthly, the formulations require that there should be a proportionate reason for permitting the evil effect. The determination of a proportionate reason is largely the task of human judgment or intuition, since precise mathematical rules can hardly be provided for establishing the relative values of the good attainable by acting and the good sacrificed by forbearing to act. Be that as it may, catholic moralists provide a number of general rules aimed at offering considerable guide in choosing or sacrificing a value in a particular situation (7).

One of such rules asserts that the intended good effect must be greater or at least as great as the effect permitted. Putting in mind that "evil" could be said to be the absence of good, this rule can be

----

7   Joseph Mausbach – Gustav Ermecke, op. cit. vol. 1, p. 258, for instance, attempt to provide such general rules when they assert: "Es muß ein entsprechend wichtiger Grund vorliegen, ein positiver persönlicher oder allgemeiner Wert oder Vorteil, der das Negative, die böse Folge aufwiegt. Das Abwägen dieses Grundes bleibt dem gewissenhaften Urteil im Einzelfall gemäß der objektiven Seins- und Wertordnung überlassen. Als Maßstab hat zu gelten: Der Grund, der positive Wert, muß um so bedeutender sein,
je schlechter die neben der guten Folge zugelassene böse Folge ist,
je näher und enger der ursächliche Zusammenhang zwischen Tat und böser Folge ist,
je wahrscheinlicher oder sicherer die böse Folge ist,
je schwächer der Rechtstitel ist, auf den der Handelnde sich berufen kann,
je mehr sonstige Rücksichten, z.B. Amts- und Berufspflichten für den Handelnden vorliegen, die Ursache nicht zu setzen oder aus dem Weg zu räumen."

restated as follows: "the desired value should at least be equivalent to the value sacrificed.". Thus, while sacrificing a human life in order to save a human life is a proportionate reason for the legitimacy of a medically indicated abortion, sacrificing a human life in order to save a person's face is not deemed a reason grave enough to permit an ethically indicated abortion.

The rule of proportionate reason is also formulated in terms of the certainty with which an evil effect is known to follow from an act. A graver reason is demanded to permit an evil effect that is certain to follow from an act than that which is merely probable to follow.

Fifthly, all the four formulations of the principle require that the evil effect should not proceed from the good. This condition is not to be understood as referring merely to the temporal priority of the effects. It rather demands that the causal chain from action to effect should exclude the case where the good is produced with the evil effect as cause. Thus to be legitimate an act should produce its effect in such a manner that either both the good and evil effects follow with equal immediacy from it or the good effect produces the evil. Were the evil effect to be causally productive of the good, the act would be morally wrong, since a good end does not justify a (morally) evil means. Thus, a therapeutic abortion to save the life of an expectant woman suffering from a heart disease is said to be morally wrong because the evil effect (death of the foetus) is the means of attaining the good effect (health of the woman). In contrast, a hysterectomy performed as a means of curing the diseased uterus of a pregnant woman is permissible because the health of the woman is not restored by the means of fetal death. Both effects proceed with equal immediacy from the act.

This condition requiring that the good effects should not proceed from the evil is in some way similar to that demanding that the act in itself should be good and often reducible to it. Both are various ways of stating the axiom: a good end does not sanctify an evil means. Which of the two applies to a given case depends on the arbitrary specification of the act-in-itself? How is the boundary between an act and its effects specified? Though moralists have a general consensus concerning this specification in most practical cases, no compelling reason is offered that provides 'a logical explanation why an act-in-itself should be specified in this manner rather than the other. The act-in-itself admits of various descriptions for various purposes. Supposing in a case of acquiring sperm for artificial insemination the act-in-itself is described as masturbation, which is deemed an intrinsic evil, then the first condition is violated. If, on the other hand, the act-in-itself is described as "fondling the genitals", the supply of sperm (good effect) follows as a result of a solitary and pleasurable emission of sperm (evil effect) then the second condition is contravened.

1.2.1.1. "The good effect should not proceed from the evil effect": A detailed appreciation

Since this condition of the principle of double effect constitutes one of the centres of attack of the rule by some modern moralists, it might be worthwhile to examine it deeper. This will be done by taking a critical glance at a few cases where this condition is applied.

It may happen that during a war a commanding officer finds it beneficial for his army to bomb the enemy's armoury in order to repel future aggressions. He carries out the operation foreseeing that it will cause the death of innocent civilians who live in the locality where the armoury is situated. It will be recalled that usually the fifth commandment is understood as prohibiting the deliberate performance of an act foreseen as bringing about the death of an innocent person. Apparently were the fifth commandment to be followed strictly the above bombing operation would be considered immoral since it causes, among other things, the death of innocent civilians. One of the reasons which catholic tradition advances for the justification of such an action which results in the death of the innocent is that the evil effect (the death of the innocent) is not intended since the good effect of repelling the aggression of the enemy is not produced by means of killing the innocent non-combatants; both the evil and good effect proceed with equal immediacy from the act (8). Thus the evil effect is not directly intended. On the other hand, were the evil effect to preceed the good effect, the killing of the innocent is described as direct killing and prohibited. Few concrete examples may help to bring these points into sharp relief.

(a)   HYSTERECTOMY

In his discussion on abortion Bernad Häring (9) relates an incident recounted to him by a gynaecologist who removed a benign uterine tumour from a woman four months pregnant. On the womb the doctor encountered numerous very thin and fragile varicose veins which bled profusely, and whose bleeding was aggravated by suturing. Two means of preventing the woman's death are available. The first consists in removing the bleeding uterus along with the fetus inhabiting it. The second lies in simply removing the fetus from the uterus whereby the bleeding would be stopped by contraction of the uterus. Death

----

8 Similarly, a doctor who intends to relieve the pains of a patient languishing in unbearable pains may administer pain-relieving drugs which he knows can shorten the life of the patient. The death of the patient is considered indirectly willed, because it proceeds from the act of administering a drug with equal immediacy as the desired reduction of pains.

9 Bernhard Häring, op. cit., vol. 3, p. 226.

of the fetus would result in either procedure. Cognizant of the fact that the fetus will not be saved in any event and believing that the preservation of the woman's fertility was desirable, the gynaecologist chose the latter procedure. He was later told by a catholic moral theologian that the alternative he chose was objectively wrong. According to the gynaecologist, "I would have been allowed to remove the bleeding uterus with the fetus itself", he said "but was not permitted to interrupt the pregnancy while leaving the womb intact. This later – he said – constituted an immoral termination of pregnancy, though done for the purpose of saving the mother, while the other would have been a lawful indirect intention and action to save life.".

It is enlightening to observe the similarity between the sanctioned act, the removal of the fetus along with the uterus, and the proscribed act, the removal of the fetus from the uterus. Both acts have the evil and undesired effect of fetal death. In addition both have the good and desired effect of preserving maternal health. However, both differ in as much as the first procedure causes more damage (namely: additional loss of material fertility) than the second which preserves the fertility of the woman. Judged from the effects they produce the second is preferable because it produces lesser harm than the first. Tradition considers the second as always prohibited, while it deems the first permissible. Why? The reason is that while the good effect (restoration of the woman's health) and the evil effect (the death of the fetus) flow immediately from the act in the first procedure, the good effect is produced by means of the evil effect in the second procedure. The second is seen as direct killing of an innocent person which is always wrong. The good ends of restoring the woman's life and preserving her fertility do not justify a wrong means.

(b)   ECTOPIC OPERATION

A somewhat similar example is provided by ectopic operation. A non-viable fetus is developing in the fallopian tube of its mother. If its development is allowed to continue the tube will rupture and the death of both mother and fetus is foreseen to follow with certainty. While no known medical procedure is able to save the child, the mother can be saved by either of two procedures. The first consists in the removal of the fetus from the tube which leaves the woman with the possibilities of future pregnancies. The second consists in the removal of the fallopian tube along with the fetus, which robs the woman of every chance of a future pregnancy. In both procedures, the operating gynaecologist has the good intention of restoring the woman's health. While the first procedure is considered absolutely forbidden by catholic tradition, the second, which produces more harmful effects, is said to be permissible. Why? The second is considered morally right because the good and evil results proceed immediately from the act itself. In contrast, the first is deemed morally wrong because the preservation of maternal fecundity (good effect) is achieved through the removal of the non-viable fetus (evil means). In this case the evil effect will be intended as a means to attaining the good one.

These examples reveal that in establishing the moral rightness and wrongness of acts that fall within the purview of the principle of double effect, Catholic tradition believes that the order by which the effects flow from the act plays a moral significant role. If both effects proceed with equal immediacy from the act or if the evil effect proceeds from the good, the act is described as "indirect" and may be permitted for a proportionate reason. In contrast, if the good effect proceeds from the evil effect, the act is considered "direct" and immoral. The reason usually advanced to prop up this teaching is given in the well-known dictum: "the end does not sanctify the means". How is this dictum to be understood?

1.2.1.2. The end does not justify the means

It is not seldom that when manuals of moral theology refer to the maxim: "The end does not sanctify the means" they support their assertion by Paul's statement in Rom. 3.8. In this text (Rom. 3.5-8), Paul attempts a sort of "reductio ad absurdum". The Jewish suggestion envisaged by him is that the Jew should not be judged by God for his infidelity because his infidelity served the noble purpose of demonstrating God's fidelity. God would be "unjust" in condemning someone whose action achieved that end. He brushes the objection aside by asserting:

> "That would be absurd, it would mean God could never judge the world. You might as well say that since my untruthfulness makes God demonstrate his truthfulness and thus gives him glory, I should not be judged to be a sinner at all. That would be the same as saying: Do evil as a means to good. Some slanderers have accused us of teaching this, but they are justly condemned." (Rom. 3.6-8).

In chapter 6 of the letter of the Romans, Paul proceeds with the same issue by asking a rhetorical question: "Does it follow that we should remain in sin so as to let grace have greater scope?" (Rom. 6.1). Paul imagines that some people may conclude from his statements in Rom. 5.15-21, that since sin gave the grace of God the opportunity to show itself in abundance therefore that chance (sin) should continue to exist in the life of Christians. Little doubt that Paul deems this a slander. After showing that by baptism a Christian dies to sin, Paul makes his stand crystal clear in Rom. 6.8-10. As Christ died once and for all to sin and now lives a life for God which knows no reversal so the Christian by baptism goes through a definitive death to sin and belongs no more to its realm. Dead to sin, the Christian lives in God through Christ. Thus it would be absurd to think that a Christian ought to sin in order that God's grace shines out.

It is quite clear from this brief exposition that Paul by employing the dictum: "a good end does not justify an evil means" in Rom. 3.8 means that a morally good end (display of God's forgiving grace) is not a sufficient reason to justify the **morally evil means** (the sin of the Jews).

This sense of the dictum does not exhaust all the possible meanings it can have because of the equivocal ways in which words like "good" and "evil" are used. A "good end" apart from signifying a "moral good end" can also depict a "non-moral good end". Similarly, an "evil means" apart from depicting a "moral evil means" can also designate a "non-moral evil means".

Assuming that the dictum attempts to indicate that it is morally wrong to do evil as a means to achieving a good end and taking into consideration the ambigious ways "good" and "evil" are used, the possible meanings, the dictum can take may thus be stated in at least four different propositions:

1.) It is morally wrong to do a moral evil as a means to achieving a moral good end.

2.) It is morally wrong to do a moral evil as a means to achieving a non-moral good end.

3.) It is morally wrong to do a non-moral evil as a means to achieving a moral good end.

4.) It is morally wrong to do a non-moral evil as a means to achieving a non-moral good end.

Taking into consideration that the meaning of "moral evil" excludes it from the realm of acts that an agent may legitimately perform, it is evident that the first and second propositions are true. "Moral evil" is an absolute disvalue that has to be avoided under every circumstance. The fact that an act is termed a "moral evil" implies that no reason can justify its performance. Thus saving one's neck during a period of religious persecution does not justify denying the faith as a means. The good end of securing a good post in government does not justify using bribery and corruption as a means.

The third proposition is evidently false. The preferential rule demands the choice of a moral value when a moral value conflicts with a non-moral value or disvalue. It is usually considered a meritorious deed if a martyr chooses death, a non-moral evil, as a means to preserving his faith. Christians perform acts of self-denial (non-moral evil) as a means of growing in faith. A "matromonium legitimum" is usually dissolved if this is the only means of safe-guarding the faith of the believing party. In all these instances a non-moral disvalue is caused as a licit means to attaining a morally good end, because there is a proportionate reason for doing so.

The fourth proposition is true in some instances and false in others. It is true in cases where a non-moral evil is caused without a proportionate grave reason. A banal example would be killing a man because he stole apples. It cannot be defended that ridding a society a thieves who appropriate other peoples' apples is a justifying reason for disposing of human life. Similarly, a tyrant cannot reasonably argue that his desire to cling fast to power entitles him to dispose of the lives of citizens who are loudly opposed to his unjust regime. These acts are deemed morally wrong because a proportionate reason is wanting.

The fourth proposition is false in cases where a non-moral good conflicts with a non-moral disvalue of equal or lesser importance. In such cases causing a non-moral disvalue is the necessary and satisfactory condition for achieving the non-moral good. The non-moral disvalue assumes the character of a "bonum utile" or "bonum propter aliud" and becomes desirable on account of the end.

Aristotle in his **Nicomachean Ethics** deals with this issue of causing a non-moral disvalue as a means to achieving a non-moral good end. He asserts:

> "A somewhat similar case is when a cargo is jettisoned in a storm; apart from circumstances, no one voluntarily throws away his property, but to save his own life and that of his shipmates any sane man would do so." (10)

This text deals with two non-moral values: material property and human life, which a person would have otherwise liked to preserve but which he cannot simultaneously do. Preserving one means sacrificing the other. The making of such choices pervades everyday life. In a shop a man exchanges his money for a good, although he usually would like to keep his money and receive the good as a gift. A student needs to burn the midnight candle to get his diploma, although responding to human inclinations he would like to receive his certificate without much labour. Such sacrificing of non-moral goods in exchange for another simply indicates that in daily life, if one wants a good he often has to pay the price.

No moralist worth the name disputes that a non-moral evil means could legitimately be used as a means to achieve a moral or non-moral good end. However, what is disputed is: which acts count for "malum morale" and which do not? It is because Catholic tradition argues that disvalues like masturbation, killing of an innocent person, the use of artificial methods of preventing conception, sterilization and the like are intrinsically evil (malum morale) that leads it to stressing that they are never to be used as a means to a good end. It is also for the same reason that it holds that an act of double effect, which produces its good effect by means of any such intrinsic evil effect, is to be considered immoral.

Anyone who holds that such disvalues are intrinsically (morally) evil makes a synthetic statement and so automatically faces the challenge of producing compelling arguments in support of his assertion. If his arguments are inconclusive, and if it established that such evils are non-moral disvalues no morally significant reason can forbid their good effect from proceeding from their non-moral evil effects if there is a proportionate reason to perform the act. The sequence of effects plays no morally relevant role, if the evil effect in question

----

10 Aristotle, **Nicomachean Ethics**, II, 1,5.

is a non-moral disvalue. This fact is revealed in everyday experience. A father spanks his child as a means of achieving some pedagogical effect. A doctor vaccinates a man as a means of making him resistant to some disease.

In a word, the proposition: the good effect should not proceed from the evil effect is only always true when the evil effect flows from a morally wrong act. The propostion is, however, not always true if the evil effect in question is a non-moral disvalue. Such an evil effect may be used as a means of producing a good effect if there is a proportionate grave reason.

1.2.1.3. Producing evil effects by means of acts of commission and acts of omission

A question related to that being discussed here is presented by the production of an evil effect by means of an act of doing, on the one hand, and by an act of allowing, on the other. A means which consists in act of "doing" and another means which consists in act of "allowing" may have exactly the same effects and the agent employing them may intend exactly the same end but while the one is considered always morally prohibited, the other is deemed morally permissible. The practice of medicine provides an apt illustration of this.

The clinical practice of medicine is frequently confronted with incurable conditions resulting from severe diseases of the heart or blood vessels producing perhaps a stroke with partial paralysis or a state of coma from which full consciousness may never be regained. By use of modern pressure respirators the (vegetative) life of the patient could be prolonged, his anguish protracted, and his family's resources drained. The question that props up in such a situation is: Should a man in such a situation be artificially kept "alive" for months or years in a fully unconscious state or in a state of obvious mental absence or great disturbance?

Some moralists defending the right of a patient to die with dignity argue that in such a situation, compassion demands that the torments of the patient should be terminated. To achieve this objective, they maintain that a doctor may administer a high dose of analgesic intended to expedite the process of death or withdraw treatment by plugging off the respirator.

Generally in considering a case of this type catholic moralists distinguish between the moral goodness or badness of the doctor's motive on the one hand, and the moral rightness or wrongness of the means (act of doing or omitting) by which he achieves his objective on the other. They argue that by acting out of compassion, the doctor performs a morally good act. However, by giving the patient a high dose of analgesic intended to kill him, the doctor acts morally wrongly. He is said to be guilty of a direct killing of an innocent person which is always morally objectionable. On the other hand, he may permitted to withdraw treatment and let the patient die.

The only difference between these two medical procedures that are differently appraised is that one is an act of "killing" (act of doing) and the other is an act of "letting-die". Is this difference morally significant? This question becomes sharper when it is recalled that a person is held responsible for the foreseen consequences resulting from his acts of commission as well as from his acts of omission. In saying the "confitoer" for instance, a penitent recalls his faults and confesses: "I have sinned ... in what I have done and in what I have failed to do". Law and morals deem a mother guilty of murder if she deliberately terminates the life of her child. Whether she does so by poisoning or starving it to death does not make her act less murderous. Presuming that one can morally perform an act by forbearing to perform a physical act, the Council Fathers declare "feed the man dying of hunger, because if you do not feed him you are killing him" (11).

It is clear that from the above instances that the distinction between "doing" and "allowing" or "killing" and "letting-die" is merely descriptive; it has no moral bite. Since killing and letting-die are ways of being responsible for a death, a norm proscribing "killing" must also prohibit "letting-die". Thus the proposition "Thou shall not kill" must be seen as including "Thou shall not let-die".

Although the distinction between "killing" and "letting-die" is descriptive, it is important to note that when faced with the alternatives of terminating the life of a terminally ill patient by means of either killing him with an over-dose of analgesic or by letting him die, one has strong aversion towards choosing the former. It is difficult to find an ethical reason to explain these divergent attitudes to these two means, which – from a practical point of view – are the same in so far as they achieve the same end. Perhaps a normal man has an (innate) inclination towards refraining from a positive act of "violence" to an innocent person.

Since human life is a great value moral norms aim at preserving it by setting limits to what harm a person can deliberately do to destroy another or himself. However, human life is not the greatest value. At times it comes into conflict with other values of equal importance, as for instance, when two human lives present themselves as alternatives which are in conflict with each other such that preserving one means destroying the other. At other times, human life comes into conflict with higher values, as for instance, when confessing one's faith stands in conflict with preserving one's life. In such instances, the former values are given preference. Thus the distinction between omission and commission could be seen as serving the purpose of setting limits to what must be done to preserve human life since life is not an absolute value.

Just as human life is disposable through acts of "doing" or "allowing" it is also preserved by means of "doing" and "allowing". Since human life is not an absolute value, one is not expected to do everything or avoid everything in order to save human life. In order to preserve human life:

----

11 Gaudium et Spes 69.

1) one is not bound to let oneself be killed by an aggressor;

2) a nation is not bound to let itself be destroyed by an aggressive neighbour;

3) a society is not bound to endure a dangerous criminal whose crime poses a threat to the common-weal.

In such cases a man or a nation uses force that is enough to defend itself even if this results in the death of a human being. Similarly, a nation at war is not bound to tolerate the aggression of soldiers of an opposing army that attacks it while using non-combatants to shield themselves. In such a case, a nation may repel the attack, even if doing so, may result in the death of innocent non-combatants.

The obligation to preserve life by acts of allowing does not stretch to these areas. In these instances one may posit an act known as resulting in death. Likewise in order to preserve life one is not expected to do everything; one may at times omit a life-saving act. When? St. Thomas Aquinas specifies the instances when the effect resulting from an act is ascribable to an agent as morally responsible for it and by so doing limits the scope where the norms demanding the preservation of human life by acts of doing is binding. He says:

> "We must take note that the cause of what follows from the failure to act is not always the agent as not acting, but only when the agent can and ought to act. For if the helmsman were unable to steer the ship, or if the ship's helm were not entrusted to him the sinking of the ship would not be attributed to him, although it might be due to his absence from the helm." (12)

To say that one is morally responsible for the evil resulting from an act of omission when one ought to act is analytically true and so communicatively empty. In the teaching of passive euthanasia catholic tradition tries to expose the range of this "ought" by distinguishing between ordinary and extraordinary means of preserving life. By his omission, a man is considered morally responsible for the death of another if, and only if, he fails to use ordinary means. On the other hand, if he fails to employ extraordinary means he is not deemed responsible for it, even though the death of the other follows from his not acting.

It is evident from the foregoing that by the distinction between "killing" and "letting-die" tradition makes a step towards interpreting the deontological prohibition of killing in a benign manner.

---

12 Thomas Aquinas, S. Th., I-II, q. 6, a. 3.

1.3. THE HISTORICAL BACKGROUND OF THE PRINCIPLE

Scholars generally share the belief that the principle of double effect was not fully formulated as found in the manuals of moral theology until the middle of the seventeeth century. However, they propound divergent opinions regarding the origin of the rule. One of the views defended is that presented by Joseph Mangan (13). Mangan argues that the principle was basically, although by no means precisely expressed in the thirteenth century by Thomas Aquinas in his discussion of killing an unjust aggressor in self defence in Summa Theologiae II-II, q. 64, a. 7. He believes that it was in reference to this teaching that such eminent sixteenth and seventeenth century theologians like Thomas de Vio Cajetan (1468-1534), Louis Molina (1536-1600), Thomas Sanches (1550-1610), and especially the Salmanticenses – preeminently Domingo de Santa Teresa (1600-1654), formulated the principle in a more precise manner. In his long article Mangan offers some rebuttal to Vincente M. Alonso's (14) contention that Thomas employs the Latin word "intendere" to refer only to the end and not to the means. He argues that Thomas does not permit the defender to intend the death of the aggressor, whether as a means or as an end. In addition he maintains that the condition of the principle which requires that the good effect should be at least equally immediate as the evil effect is found in Thomas' treatment of killing an aggressor in self defence. He illustrates this by referring to Thomas' statement in the context which he translates as "it is wrong

_____

13 Joseph T. Mangan, S.J., "An Historical Analysis of the Principle of Double Effect", Theological Studies X (1949), p. 41-46. The following authors share Mangan's view: T. Lincoln Bouscaren, S.J., **Ethics of Ectopic Operations** (Milwaukee: Bruce Publishing co. 1944) pp. 31-34. Paul Ramsey, **War and the Christian Conscience**, (Durhan, North Carolina: Duke University Press 1961), pp. 34-59. Peter Knauer, "The Hermeneutic Function of the Principle of Double Effect", in: **Readings in Moral Theology No. 1**, (ed. Charles Curran and Richard McCormick, New York, Paulist Press 1979), p. 3.

14 Alonso, in his dissertation, **El principio doble efecto en los comentadores de Sancto Thomas de Aquino** (Romae 1937), argues that the principle of double effect was not enuntiated by Thomas in S. Th., II.II, q. 64, a. 7. He studies Thomas' use of "intendere" in the light of the opinions of St. Thomas' predeccessors and contemporaries, and in the light of Thomas' other works and arrives at the conclusion that Thomas applies it consistently to refer to the end.

for a man to intend to kill another as a means to defend himself."(15)

One simple question which authors that share Mangan's view have so far failed to answer effectively is: if the principle has its origin in St. Thomas' discussion on self defence against an unjust aggressor, why is it that the principle is not employed by catholic tradition in justifying killing in self defence? Some of the eminent authors (16), whom Mangan associates with, the formulation of the principle, expressly assert that the principle is not necessary for the justification of killing in self-defence and maintain that it is licit to intend to kill an unjust aggressor when doing so is the only way of preserving one's life.

The second opinion regarding the origin of the principle of double effect is that proposed by J. Ghoos (17). Ghoos asserts that the principle is in no way entailed in St. Thomas's treatment of killing an aggressor in self defence. He believes that the origin of the principle was stimulated by an endeavour to unite two realities that were distinct in the writings of St. Thomas, namely, "the indirect voluntary" and "voluntarium in causa". Thomas uses the first to refer to an effect that comes about by the failure to act (S. Th. I-II, q. 6, a. 3.). The second term, "voluntary in its cause", is employed by Thomas in referring to an effect that was willed not in itself but in its cause (S. Th., I.II, q. 77, a. 7). Ghoos maintains that both terms gradually became syonymous with each other in the course of the sixteenth and seventeenth centuries and assumed the meaning which "voluntarium in causa" had in the writings of Thomas Aquinas. Furthermore, he asserts that the precise formulation was the work of John of St. Thomas (1589–1644) in his De bonitate et malitia actum humanorum.

Although authors are disagreeded on the precise origin of the principle of double effect, no one, however, contends that the prin-

----

15 J. Mangan, op.cit., p. 48.
   On this issue Charles Curran, Ongoing Revision in Moral Theology, Notre Dame 1965, p. 176 disagrees utterly with Mangan. He asserts: "It is somewhat difficult to see how such a translation could prove that in the order of physical causality the killing of the aggressor cannot be a means of defend one's life ... Thus in my judgement Mangan does not prove that the accepted notion of double effect, expecially with its third condition, is found in Aquinas."

16 Ludovicus Molina, S.J., De justitia et jure, (Moguntiae 1659), t. 4, tr. 3, disp. 11; Dominicus de Soto, O.P., De justitia et jure, (Salamantica 1556), 1.5, q. 1, a. 8; Leonardus Lessius, De justitia et jure, (Mediolani 1613), 1.2, c. 9, dub. 8, n. 53; Gabriel Vasquez, S.J. Opuscula morali, (Ludguni 1620), "De restitutione", c. 3, par. 1, dub. vi.

17 J. Ghoos, "L'acte à double effet Etude de Théologie positive", in: Ephemerides Theologicae Lovaniensis, 27, (1951), p. 30-52. It is instructive to note that eminent theologians like Lessius, Soto and Vasquez, in the texts cited above, are of the opinion that the principle of double effect does not originate from Thomas' treatment of killing in self-defence.

ciple was in use before its explicit formulation. John Mangan believes he can trace the application of the principle back to the Old Testament. He instances 1 Maccabees 6 as a striking example where the principle was employed in the justification of self-killing. In this text Eleazar, a Jew, was fighting in the army of the opposing Maccabees against an enemy force. Identifying an elephant on which he believed the king of the opposing side was riding to battle, Eleazar ran under it and slew it, knowing that he would be crushed, but hoping that he would thus kill the king or at least disable him. The inspired narrative presents this act as something commendable.

There is ample evidence that the principle was extensively used in the sixteenth and seventeenth centuries. Francisco de Vitoria (18), Franciscus Suarez (19), Leonardus Lessius (20), Paul Layman (21), Gregorius de Valentina (22) apply it in justifying the killing of the innocent, particularly, during the period of war. Suarez (23), Layman (24), Lessius (25), Valentina (26), and Becanus (27) employ it in justifying the performance of an act foreseen to result in scandal. Thomas Sanchez (28), Layman (29), Ludovicus Molina (30) and Valentia (31) use the principle in approving actions involving cooperation

----

18 Francisco de Vitoria O.P., **Comentarios a la Secunca Secundae de Sancto Tomas** (Editio praeparanda por el R.P. Vincente Beltram de Heredia O.P., Salamanca 1934), II-II, q. 64, a. 6, n. 6.

19 Franciscus Suarez, S.J. **Opera Omnia,** ed. Carolus Berton (Parisiis 1856 sq)' t. 12, tr. 3, disp. 13, sect. 7, n. 15-19.

20 Leonardus Lessius, S.J., op. cit. 1.2. c. 9, dub. 7 no 36 ff.; and n. 57-59; 1.2. c 9, dub. 10, n. 62.

21 Paul Laymann, S.J., **Theologia Moralia** (Monachii, Heinrich 1626) 1,2, tr. 3, c. 12, n. 11,12.

22 Gregorius de Valentia, S.J., **Commentariorum Theologicorum** (Benetiis 1605), t. 3, disp. 5, q. 8, punct. 2, n. 1063, 1064; disp. 3, q. 16, punct. 3, n. 785 A.

23 Franciscus Suarez, S.J. op. cit., t. 12, tr. 3, disp. 10, sect. 3,4.

24 Paul Laymann, S.J., op. cit., 1,2. tr. 3, c. 13, n. 8 ff.

25 L. Lessius, op. cit. 1.4, c. 4, dub. 14, n. 113,114.

26 Gregorius de Valentina, S.J., op. cit. t. 3, disp. 3, q. 18, punct. 4, n. 818, D,E.

27 M. Becanus, **De fide, spe et caritate,** (Lugduni 1626), "de scandalo", q. 6.

28 Thomas Sanchez, S.J., De praeceptis decalogi (Viterbi 1738), I.1, c. 7, n. 8-18.

29 Paul Laymann, S.J., op. cit., 1.2, tr. 3, c. 13, n. 4,8.

30 Ludovicus Molina, S.J., op. cit., t. 1, tr. 2, disp. 115, n. 4.

31 Gregorius de Valentia, S.J., op. cit., t. 3, disp. 1, q. 10, punct. 5.

in the sin of others. Likewise Sanchez (32), Lessius (33), John Wiggers (34), Valentia (35) and the Salmanticenses (36) apply the principle in justifying the performance of acts foreseen to result in self-pollution.

Following the footsteps of these moralists of the sixteenth and seventeenth centuries moral theology handbooks employ the principle in resolving moral dilemmas involving scandal, cooperation in the sin of others, sterilization, use of contraceptive devices, masturbation and the killing of an innocent person (suicide, homicide).

The use of this principle is not a special preserve of moral theologians. A series of popes employ the principle in making decisive statements on vexing moral questions. Pope Pius XI, for instance, employs the direct/indirect distinction, which stands at the core of the principle, in his discussion of abortion. He asks "what could ever be a sufficient reason for excusing in any way the direct murder of the innocent?" (37) Likewise, Pope XII applies the principle in his treatment of sterilization. He observes:

> "If the wife takes his medication not with a view to preventing conception, but solely on the advice of a physician, as a necessary remedy by reason of a malady of the uterus or of the organism, she is causing indirect sterilization which remains permissible according to the general principle concerning actions having a double effect. But one causes a direct sterilization, and therefore an illicit one, whenever one stops ovulation in order to preserve the uterus and the organism from the consequences of a pregnancy which they are not able to stand." (38)

Similarly, Pope Paul VI explicitly employs this distinction in his teaching on birth regulation and sterilization in **Humanae Vitae.** He maintains:

> "Therefore we base our words on the first principles of human and Christian doctrine of marriage when we are obliged once more to declare that the direct interruption

----

32 Thomas Sanchez, S.J., **De sancto matrimonii sacramento** (Venetiis 1712), 1.9, disp. 45, nn. 4-32.

33 Leonardus Lessius, op. cit., 1.4, c. 3, dub. 8, n. 60,65.

34 John Wiggers, **De jure et justitia** (Lovanii 1651), "De temperantia", c. 3, dub. 12, n. 65,70.

35 Valentia, S.J., op. cit., t. 3, disp. 9, q. 3, punct. 3, n. 1813, C,D.

36 Salamanticenses, **Cursus Theologicus** (Parisiis, Bruxellis 1877), t. 7, tr. 13, disp. 10, dub. 6, n. 211 ff.

37 AAS, 22, (1930): 563

38 AAS, 50, (1958): 753-56

of the generative process already begun and, above all, direct abortion, even for therapeutic reasons, are to be absolutely excluded as lawful means of controlling the birth of children. Equally to be condemned, as the Magisterium of the church has affirmed on various occasions, is direct sterilization, whether of the man or of the woman, whether permanent or temporary." (39)

To sum up, it is important to note that although the wording of the principle of double effect does not show in a crystal clear manner whether the rule is applicable to all cases where evil results from an act or not, historical evidence portrays that catholic moral theologians of celebrated name as well as the magisterium have applied it exclusively to acts productive of the so called intrinsic (moral) evil. No evidence is available of its application to acts which produce physical evil (malum physicum).

---

39 Humanae Vitae, (London C.T.S. 1968), no. 14.

2.

THE CHARACTER OF ACTS GOVERNED BY THE PRINCIPLE OF DOUBLE EFFECT

In his reevaluation of the traditional presentation of the principle of double effect, Bruno Schüller remarks that: "It is comparatively easy to apply this principle correctly, but extremely difficult to give a satisfactory account of its meaning and validity." (1) To my mind part of the difficulties entailed in understanding this principle is largely due to the complicated character of the acts that fall within the ambient of its application. First, while some of these acts produce their effects with some sort of intrinsic necessity, others generate theirs in a manner that may be described as accidental. Second, each of these acts appears to have a double moral character, if one be permitted to assess an act morally from the results it produces. In so far as an act of this group produces a good effect, it may be described as morally right and permissible. In contrast, in so far as it generates intrinsic (moral) evil, it is deemed morally wrong and thus always prohibited. Accordingly, acts governed by the principle of double effect appear to be morally permissible and at the same time always morally proscribed. A closer examination of these acts from the point of view of these peculiar characteristics may help to shed more light in understanding the principle in its pristine formulation and traditional application.

2.1. THE PRINCIPLE OF DOUBLE EFFECT APPLICABLE TO TWO DIFFERENT KINDS OF CAUSES

2.1.1. ACTION UNDERSTOOD AS A CAUSE: AN ILLUSTRATION

In analysing the constituents of a given human performance the question that has perplexed philosophers of action is how to draw a boundary between an action and its consequences. Where does an action terminate and where do its consequences begin? In a question regarding the event of killing, for instance, it may be asked what did X do when he killed Y? In reply to this question the following act-descriptions are possible:

a) He tensed his finger;

b) He pressed the trigger of a gun;

----

1   B. Schüller, "The Double Effect in Catholic Thought: a Reevaluation", in: McCormick and Ramsey, ed., **Doing Evil to Achieve Good**, Chicago, Loyola University Press, 1978, p. 166.

c) He fired a gun;

d) He shot at Y;

e) He killed Y.

If "a" is the act-description, then all the events stretching from "b" to "e" are classifiable as its effects. If "d", on the other hand, is chosen as the act-description, then only "e" is describable as the effect of the action (2). What constitutes that part of an action which is called effect varies. It largely depends on what elements of an event are included in the act-description (3). Thus in the description of a human performance a man could classify an element as part of the action, while another considers it a part of the consequence (4).

However, irrespective of what elements are included in an act-description, the statement: "A causes that E", whereby "A" is the name of the cause and "E" the description of the effect, is an acceptable act-description. Thus an action is designated as a cause in so far as every (commanded) act is prone to producing some effects. In the common parlance of legal philosophers the causality of the agent's deed is said to "reach through" events subsequent to it to other and more remote events (5). Be that as it may, neither in law nor in common morality can it be defended that the causal "reach" of an action can extend to every subsequent event that would not have occurred had the action not been posited. In this regard, two illustrations by Hart and Honoré have become classical examples:

I) "A forest fire breaks out, and later investigations show that shortly before the outbreak A had flung away a lightened cigarette into the bracken at the edge of the forest, the bracken cought fire, a light breeze got up, and faned the flames in the direction of the forest." (6)

----

2 With some modifications this illustration is taken from Eric d'Arcy, **Human Acts**, Oxford Clarendon Press 1969, p. 3.

3 On this point Andrew Oldenquist's remark is enlightening. He says: "There is ... no rigid distinction between action and consequence, and we are free to construe many characteristics either as results or as constitutive of an expanded version." Cf. Choosing, Deciding, Doing", in: Paul Edwards, ed., **The Encyclopedia of Philosophy**, vol. 2, London 1972, p. 101.

4 The flexibility in act-description seems to be one of the sources of the disagreement between deontologists and teleologists. It is not seldom that the former include a wrong-making-property in their description of an act and so maintain that an act is wrong without reference to its consequences while teleologists classify the same property as part of the act's effects and so assert that effects always play a significant role in the moral evaluation of an act.

5 H.L.A. Hart and A.M. Honoré, **Causation in Law**, Oxford, Clarendon Press 1959, pp. 67-69.

6 Hart and Honoré, ibid., p. 67.

II) "A throws a lighted cigarette into the bracken which catches fire. B, just as the flames are about to flicker out, deliberately pours petrol on them. The fire spreads and burns down the forest." (7)

In both cases, the human performance describable as "the throwing by A of lighted cigarette into the bracken" is one of a set of conditions necessary for the breaking-out of fire. If it had not taken place, the fire would not have broken out. Yet only in the first case can A's action is throwing the cigarette be correctly described as the cause of the fire. Why?

An action, as understood in law, is a deed by a human agent performed in a particular situation or in a set of circumstances. This deed could either consist in an intervention in a natural process (act of doing) or in an abstention from intervention (act of omission). When he intervenes, he can be described as causing whatever would not have occured had he abstained; and when he abstains, as allowing to happen whatever would not have happened had he intervened. The agent is like a "deus ex machina", whose intervention makes the difference to what otherwise would not naturally have come about. In this conception of action, it does not matter in case (I), whether or not the agent believed, intended or hoped that a breeze would get up, and fan the flames kindled by his cigarette, or that the forest fire would follow. What determines whether his throwing away his cigarette was the cause of the fire is simply whether, his situation being what it was, the outbreak of fire followed from his deed in the course of nature.

Ruled out from this understanding of action considered from the aspect of cause and effect are abnormal occurrences which intervene to break the chain of causation from action to effect. Such abnormal occurrence is exemplified by B's intervention, an event seen as a second action or to put it in the legal parlance a "novus actus interveniens". This causal influence of the previous action cannot be said to extend to it.

2.1.2. THE PRINCIPLE APPLICABLE TO CAUSA PER SE

In a somewhat related but different way catholic tradition treats human action as cause under the categories of "causa per se" and "causa per accidens". A few examples will help to illuminate what catholic moralists understand by these terms. It is an established scientific fact that progesterone compounds cause temporary sterility in a woman. The taking of this compound by a woman is an action, which by its nature tends to cause sterility, is known as a "causa per se". Thus a cause which tends by its nature to produce an effect such that the effect proceeds from the placed cause with a sort of physical necessity is known as "causa per se" or a natural cause.

----

7 Hart and Honoré, ibid., p. 69.

The effect, sterility, proceeding from the act of taking the compounds is termed "effectus per se" or a "necessary effect" or a "natural effect". Acts governed by the principle of double effect that fall within the purview of acts described as "causa per se" include acts of killing, sterilization, the use of contraceptive devices and the like.

An act which produces a double (per se) effect is well illustrated by an act of bombing during a war. A military pilot in order to ward off further unjust aggression of the enemy drops a bomb on the latter's military installations, which simultaneously causes the destruction of some military equipment (good effect) and the lives of some non-combatants who live in the vicinity (evil effect). Both effects are said to proceed as "per se" or natural effects from the act of bombing which is a "causa per se". Although he is the physical cause of both "per se" effects, he is not considered the moral cause of the evil effect if he complies to the prescriptions of the principle of double effect. Where he fails to comply to this rule, as for instance, where he also intends to kill the non-combatants as a way of demoralizing the enemy-soldiers, he is then considered the moral cause of the evil effect and so morally accountable for it.

2.1.3. THE PRINCIPLE APPLICABLE TO CAUSE PER ACCIDENS

In contrast to "causa per se", a causa may not tend by its nature to produce a particular effect but may, on the other hand, provide the occasion for the production of some effect. Such a cause is referred to as "causa per accidens". The effect occasioned by it is known as "effectus per accidens" or an accidental effect. Acts of scandal and cooperation in the sin of another governed by the principle of double effect fall within the scope of "causa per accidens". The following are classical illustrations.

1) A man (A) intending to ravage a virgin needs someone to hold a ladder suspended to a wall of a house in order to climb in through the window to get at his victim. His friend (B) did him the service. Thanks to B's aid (cooperatio necessarius) A accomplishes his sinful designs. A's sinful action in as much as it follows from B's cooperating act is described as an accidental effect. B's cooperating act is said to be a "causa per accidens" in relation to A's sin.

2) B, an exemplary and highly influencial Christian, lives in an area where Christians are permitted to eat meat on Friday. His friend, A, who comes from an area strictly obliged by the law of abstinence, visits B and watches him enjoy meat on Friday. He takes scandal and on his return home begins to eat meat on Friday in defiance of the existing law of abstinence in his place of residence.

In each of the two cases B's sin is described as "effectus per accidens" in reference to A's act which is a "causa per accidens". It is evident that the act of holding a ladder or eating of meat on Friday do not by their nature give rise to sin. For sin to result from them the intervention of a free agent is necessary (8). In the eyes of philosophers of action as has been shown above, such an intervention breaks the chain of causation from action to effect. Thus B's sin in either of the example can not be strictly described as an effect of A's action, nor can A's action be strictly be said to be the cause of B's.

Sin, by its nature, results from the deliberate and free decision of a person to perform a morally objectionable act. Thus strictly speaking it can not be said to be the result of the action of a second party. A second party can, at worst, provide the occasion of sin as is the case in the example of scandal. However, it is worthwhile to note that an occasion of sin for B can also be seen as an occasion of grace for him. He could freely resist the temptation to sin and thereby win grace. Be that as it may, in a wide sense A could be said to be the cause (causa occasionalis) of the sinful act of B in as much as the latter would not have taken the decision to sin had A abstained from eating meat on Friday.

How far could B's cooperating act in the first example be rightly described as causing A's sin? Framing the question in a different way, how can A's sin be said to result from B's act of cooperation? A's sin consists first and foremost in his deliberate and free decision to ravage a virgin. This sinful decision is prior to his search for the helping hand of B. Thus B, by cooperating, cannot be said to be the cause of A's sin that is already existing before his intervention. His refraining from helping in the circumstances would not have impeded A's sin. At best it could have prevented the resulting harm done to the virgin.

2.2. THE PRINCIPLE OF DOUBLE EFFECT AS APPLYING TO ACTS WITH AN APPARENT DOUBLE MORAL CHARACTER

The traditional presentation of the principle of double effect as a rule that justifies or prohibits the performance of an act with a twofold effect, one good, the other evil, has something unsatisfactory and misleading about it. It fails to indicate in an unequivocal manner what type of evil is under reference and thereby creates room for misunderstanding. One, who is not well acquainted with the use of the principle by catholic moralists might imagine that the rule applies to every case where good and evil proceed from an action. No. One insight gained from the historical survey of the concrete application of the principle is that in the catholic tradition moralists consistently restrict its use exclusively to solving moral dilemmas involving an act which simultaneously causes a good and an intrinsic (moral) evil.

---

8 Cf. A. Vermeersch, "De causalitate per se et per accidens", Periodica, XXI, (1932), p.109.

It is necessary to note that apart from intrinsic (moral) evil catholic tradition knows of non-moral or physical evils (malum physicum) like deception, pain, amputation, loss of repute, loss of property and the like. In justifying the causation of such evils catholic tradition does not usually employ the principle of double effect. Rather it appeals to the principle of proportionate reason or preferential principle (choosing of the lesser evil, the principle of totality and so on·). Catholic moralists teach, for instance, that a person starving to death may take somebody else's food to still his hunger. This act which produces two effects – loss of property and saving of a human life – is not justifiable because it meets the demands of the principle of double effect, but because there is a proportionate reason for causing the loss of property. It suffices to stress here that catholic moralists consider the existence of proportionate reason a justification for the causing of physical (non-moral) evil. On the other hand, for the causation of an intrinsic (moral) evil, it demands more than a proportionate reason, it requires the fulfilment of the prescriptions of the principle of double effect.

If one were to establish the moral rightness or wrongness of acts from the values and disvalues they produce, the acts governed by the principle of double effect will appear to have a double moral character. For instance, when one considers the performance of hysterectomy on an expectant woman from the non-moral values it produces, that is to say, in so far as it restores the woman's health, the procedure may be described as morally right. Conversely, when one views it from the disvalue or intrinsic (moral) evil it brings about, that is to say, in so far as it causes the death of an innocent child, one following the catholic tradition will consider it morally wrong. Thus the principle of double effect applies to actions which seem simultaneously morally permitted and always proscribed.

If an act governed by the principle of double effect is to be legitimately performed, one of the questions that necessarily arises is: which of the elements of the action, namely, a) cause (understood as an action), b) the good effect, c) the evil effect, may be intended? In replying to this question, it is necessary to note that if two ends (effects) are attainable only by one means (act), intending to achieve either or both ends (effects) ipso facto entails intending the single and necessary means (act). In this regard it is worthwhile to recall the scholastic maxim which asserts that "He who intends the end intends also the necessary means to it". If either the good or the bad effect is intended, the cause or act, seen as a means to achieving it, will always be intended. Thus in so far as the act is considered a "cause", an agent cannot but will it, at least, as a "causa quae causa" if he intends to achieve either of the effects. In this case there is no choice between willing and not willing the act; it simply has to be willed. However, in so far as it is productive of twofold effects, it could be willed as "causa qua causa" in respect to either effects, such that by intending the effect the act is also intended.

The question is then: apart from intending the act or cause which of the two effects may one intend in order to act in a morally unobjectionable manner? Here tradition answers: the good effect alone should be intended; the evil effect may never be intended. Taking it as obvious that by intending the good end (effect) the necessary means (act) to attaining it is also intended, tradition perhaps finds it necessary only to stress that the evil effect should never be intended. By doing this, room is created for misunderstanding. One may consequently, draw the conclusion that, since one may never intend the evil effect, it is deemed a moral (intrinsic) evil by tradition (9). No, tradition does not consider an evil effect such as the death of an innocent person an intrinsic (moral) evil; moral evil are predicated of human acts and not of their effects. What it considers an intrinsic (moral) evil in this respect is the **act** of killing an innocent person. It is such an act that should never be intended.

From the foregoing it is evident that the principle of double effect does not apply to every act which produces two effects, good and evil. Its use is rather restricted to an act with a double moral character, an act that may be said to be right in so far as it produces a value and always wrong in so far as it produces an intrinsic (moral) evil.

2.3. THE PRINCIPLE APPLICABLE TO ACTS DIFFERENTLY NORMED

This principle, in as much as it deals with intrinsic (moral) evil acts, is an offshoot of the teaching of traditional manuals on the "Fontes moralitatis" (10). In this extremely difficult tract manuals maintain that an act receives its moral character primarily from its object, that is to say from its "finis operis", and secondarily from its end (finis operantis) and circumstances. An act which is intrinsically evil (morally wrong) in its object cannot be made right by reason of its good circumstances or good end (finis operantis). "Bonum ex integra causa, malum ex quocumque defectu". Why does tradition consider an object an intrinsic (moral) evil? Of the reasons offered three are relevant to acts governed by the Principle of double effect. One of these reasons is teleological; the other two are deontological. What are the reasons?

---

9 Felix M. Podimattan, **Relativity of Natural Law in the Renewal of Moral Theology**, Rome 1969, p. 155 says "The principle of double effect seems to us to be redundant. It has a serious weak point. It takes for granted that of two effects that result from an act, one is morally good and the other morally evil". This statement represents a typical misunderstanding of the nature of the acts governed by the principle of double effect. It must be stressed that only acts can be described as morally right or wrong. Strictly speaking, effects are only bearers of non-moral values.

10 In the course of this work when an act is said to be an intrinsic evil, it has to be understood as morally evil from its object as found in the tract on the "fontes moralitatis".

2.3.1. THE RULE APPLICABLE TO ACTS TELEOLOGICALLY NORMED

In the tract on the "fontes moralitatis" catholic tradition may deem an object or act an intrinsic (moral) evil because of the consequences it produces, namely, because its performance constitutes an immediate danger to sin. Active scandal and cooperation in the sin of the other governed by the principle of double effect fall within this class.

"Scandalum activum" which consists in an act which is not sinful in itself, but which is nevertheless apparently sinful is forbidden by Tradition because of its possible consequence of arousing an uninformed or a weak onlooker into sin, that is to say, because it can result in "scandalum pusillorum". An illustration of this could be provided by the case of a couple living in a canonically invalid marriage because one or both parties had had a valid "matrimonium ratum et consummatum" before, but whose parish priest for some reason grants permission to receive the sacraments, as for instance, because they solemnly promised to live as brother and sister. This couple may cause scandal were they to receive the sacraments in their parish church where they are known to be cohabiting without been validly married. For this reason they are obliged to receive the sacraments in a church where they are unknown. Thus the reception of the sacraments in a church where they are known is judged morally objectionable because of the scandal foreseen to result from this act which is otherwise morally unobjectionable.

It is easy to see that material cooperation in the sin of the other, just as "scandalum activum" is normed teleologically. Usually it is generally considered morally wrong to render material assistance to a robber. But a salesman, for instance, is deemed permitted to hand over the key of a safe to a robber who threatens to shoot him to death if he fails to comply to his orders of surrendering the key. In this case two disvalues, loss of life and loss of property, are weighed. Since the loss of life is considered the greater of the two non-moral evils, the preference rule requires that it has to be avoided.

2.3.2. THE RULE APPLIES TO ACTS DEONTOLOGICALLY NORMED

In the tract on the "fontes moralitatis" Tradition may also deem an act an intrinsic (moral) evil because it is said to be performed without the required authorization (ex defectu juris in agente). Such is said to be the case with the killing of an innocent person (suicide, homicide) and mutilation of one's members. Both acts are governed by the principle of double effect. In norming these acts Tradition argues that man is only a caretaker of his body and so has no right to dispose of it or of its members. Only God, who is Lord over life and death, has the prerogative of doing so. A man who, for instance, kills an innocent person acts beyond his powers and as it were arrogates to himself the inalienable right of God.

Tradition may also consider an act an intrinsic (moral) evil because it frustrates the finality of a natural (God-given) faculty. The use of artificial contraceptive devices and the practice of masturbation governed by the principle of double effect fall within this group. In norming these acts tradition argues that God equiped man with the sexual organs for the purpose of propagating offspring. Accordingly each sexual act should be left open to achieving this end. Attempts at impeding the achievement of this end by using contraceptive devices or by onanism are thus said to be against nature or God's will.

It is evident that in the moral appraisal of these groups of acts Tradition does not take the effects they produce into consideration. In the eyes of Tradition, for instance, no imaginable beneficial results would make an intentional killing of an innocent person morally right.

From the foregoing it is to be concluded that the principle of double effect applies to acts with an apparent double moral character, that is to say, it governs acts that can be judged morally right because of the values they produce and at the same time morally wrong because of the moral disvalues (intrinsic evil) they bring into existence. Judged from the manner by which intrinsic evil effects proceed from them and from the way they are morally appraised in Catholic tradition, they reveal essential differences. On the one hand, they are constituted by acts which are "causae per se" and which tradition appraises deontologically, on the other hand, they embrace acts which are "causae per accidens" and which are assessed teleologically by Catholic tradition.

3

THE DIRECT/INDIRECT DISTINCTION OF THE PRINCIPLE
OF DOUBLE EFFECT

The direct/indirect distinction permeates the doctrine of double effect and appears to play some significant roles in the moral appraisal of acts governed by the principle of double effect. This distinction is based on the causal relationship of the effects of the acts well as to the intention of the agent. If the good effect is productive of the evil effect or if both follow from the act immediately or independent of each other, the act is described as "indirect"; this is permitted for a proportionate reason. If, in contrast, the good is produced through the means of the evil, the act is deemed "direct" and always proscribed. This is because the evil effect will be intended as a means to producing the intended good. Intending the evil effect is considered always evil.

It is easy to see that this distinction plays a morally significant role when it is applied to scandal and cooperation in the sin of others. For instance, since leading one into sin (scandal) is in itself sinful, the proposition: "You ought not intend to scandalize your neighbour", is **analytic.** Sin is an absolute (moral) disvalue and so "ex definitione" its forming the object of the will's intention is forbidden. Thus between direct scandal (intending to lead another into sin) and indirect scandal (not intending to lead another into sin) there exists some morally significant difference.

It is the application of the direct/indirect distinction to acts appraised deontologically that generated much of the current discussion over the relevance of the principle of double effect. Statements like: "You ought not kill an innocent person" or "You ought not use artificial methods to prevent conception" are **synthetic.** The reason for these proscriptions demands further clarification from the one who makes them. If, for instance, it is true that one should not kill an innocent person because killing him is in itself an absolute (moral) disvalue, that is to say, the causing of a moral disvalue, it is easy to see why intending to kill an innocent person is morally wrong. In such a case the distinction between direct and indirect killing of an innocent person will be morally significant.

If, on the other hand, it is seen that killing an innocent person is the causing of a non-moral disvalue, which however becomes a moral evil for want of a proportionate reason, does the distinction still have a moral bite or is it to be seen as merely descriptive? If it is only descriptive should it be abandoned as useless?

This chapter will be devoted to answering these questions. First, it will be shown that the distinction between direct/indirect in so far as it means "intending" and "not-intending" moral disvalue plays a morally significant role. To demonstrate this the direct/indirect distinction will be applied to scandal and cooperation in the sin of others, acts which are in themself sinful and which are appraised teleologically by catholic tradition. Second, it will be revealed that the distinction plays only a descriptive role when it signifies "willing" and "not willing" a non-moral disvalue. Here attempts will be made to show that acts deontologically normed by Tradition are non-moral evil producing. Finally it will also be demonstrated, by recourse to historical evidence, that the distinction serves tradition the use of a restrictive interpretation on deontological norms.

3.1. DIRECT/INDIRECT AS APPLICABLE TO ACTS TELEOLOGICALLY JUDGED

3.1.1. SCANDAL

To appreciate the moral relevance of the direct/indirect distinction as it is applied by moral handbooks to assessing acts of scandal, it is necessary to have a nodding acquaintance with some technical terms like scandal, active and passive scandal frequently used in this tract.

3.1.1.1. Notion of scandal

Scandal is derived from the Greek "skandalon" which depicts a trap, a hindrance or that which causes a fall. It is a word with a wide range of meaning. In a popular sense it signifies an objective act, person or thing that offends or shocks the moral feelings of people. Thus, it could be said that the slum area of a large city is a scandal. Sometimes the word 'scandal' is used in a subjective sense to refer to the reaction of people at knowing the shameful or discreditable deed of another. In this sense the word is used to refer not so much to the person or act that causes the shame but to the reaction itself. In this sense a decent citizen might be said to take scandal at the sight of a slum.

In the handbooks of moral theology, scandal signifies not so much something shameful and therefore likely to cause a reaction of indignation and outrage, but something that provides occasion and incitement to the sin of another. Most manuals following the footprints of St. Thomas Aquinas (1) define it as "verbum vel factum minus rectum, praebens alteri occasionem ruinae spiritualis" (2).

Scandal, understood as "verbum et factum" consists in something external; be it word (order, encouragement, persuasion, advice), behaviour (particularly a suggestive action) or even omission which can

----

1 cf. S. Th. II-II, q. 43, a. 1.

2 F. Regatillo and M. Zalba, op. cit., vol. 1, pp. 896-897.

provide occasion of sin for the other. When scandal is said to have the character of "minus rectum" it is understood as a word or an act or an omission which is either morally wrong in itself or which has the appearance of a morally wrong act. Circumstances could make an act, which is otherwise not morally objectionable, appear morally wrong. The eating of meat on Friday in an area dispensed from the law of abstinence could, for instance, appear morally wrong to an uninformed observer.

Usually passive scandal (scandalum passivum) is distinguished from active scandal (scandalum activum). Passive scandal or the taking of scandal consists in sinning as a result of an incitement from another. Since it could be occasioned by a sinful act or an act only sinful in appearance, "scandalum datum" is distinguished from "scandalum acceptum". It is called "scandalum datum" when it proceeds from a wrong or sinful action of another. It is termed "scandalum acceptum" if it results from an act of another which is not morally objectionable in itself.

Following the foot-steps of Thomas Aquinas (3), manuals distinguish further between "scandalum pusillorum" and "scandalum pharisaicum" in their treatment of passive scandal. When the resulting scandal is due to ignorance or infirmity, it is described as "scandalum pusillorum" or scandal of the weak. Paul refers to this sort of scandal in his letter to the Romans. In this letter he agrees with the enlightened members of the Church of Rome that all food is clean. Nevertheless, he admonishes them to abstain from meat and wine and anything else that could make a brother fall (cf. Rom. 14:20-21). Reference to this species of scandal is also evident in the First Letter to the Corinthians. While addressing the knowledgeable Christians in Corinth who felt themselves free to eat food offered to idols, Paul urges them to desist from eating such, if their insisting on "knowledge could become the ruin of someone weak, a brother for whom Christ died" (1 Cor. 8:11).

When the taking of scandal results from malice, it is described as pharisaic scandal (scandalum pharisaicum). In this case scandal is taken from an act not morally objectionable. Thus the taking of scandal is simply due to malice of the one who sins. The sinner wrests on the right action of another to his own hurt by preserve misconstruction. Pharisaic scandal takes its name from the Pharisees who consistently took scandal from Christ's work of benevolence (cf. Mt. 12:9, 14; Lk. 13:10-17).

In contradistinction to Passive scandal or the taking of scandal there is Active Scandal or the giving of scandal. Active scandal, which could occur with or without the taking of scandal, consists in performing or omitting an act, sinful in itself or in appearance that could incite one's neighbour to sin. The definition of scandal found in handbooks usually refers to this type of scandal. Moreover, the direct/indirect distinction used in the moral evaluation of the act of scandal is applied to scandal of this class.

----

3 S. Th. II-II, q. 43, a. 7.

3.1.1.2. Direct/indirect scandal

Calling to mind that active scandal can arise from a sinful or an apparently sinful act and also recalling that passive scandal can be "scandalum pharisaicum" or "scandalum pusillorum" an act of active scandal and its results may be understood in different senses:

1) A sinful act is performed and "scandalum pusillorum" follows as a result.

2) An apparently sinful act (or right act) is performed and "scandalum pusillorum" follows as a result.

3) An apparently sinful act (or a right act) is performed and "scandalum pusillorum" follows as a result

The moral character of the first act is "per se nota". Sin "ex definitione" designates an act that should never be performed. The guilt of a giver of scandal increases if he foresees that his morally objectionable act will lead a weak spectator astray and, nevertheless performs it. Accordingly Christ sternly warns: "It is impossible that snares to sin should not arise; but woe to him through whom they do arise? It would be better for him if a millstone were hung around his neck and he were thrown into the sea rather than he should cause one of these little ones to trip up" (Lk 17:1-2).

Just as the first, the assessment of the second case does not present any difficulty. The performance of an apparently sinful act (or a right act) when scandal pharisaicum is foreseen to follow is justifiable for a proportionate reason (4).

It is the assessment of acts similar to the third case that gives rise to difficult problems. It is evident that providing the occasion of sin for a "weak" or "ignorant" brother is an offence against charity (5). Charity obliges a man to assist his neighbour in his temporal needs. It obliges him still more strongly to refrain from being the source of his neighbour's spiritual harm.

Since the giver of scandal who posits an act apparently sinful is deemed responsible for the foreseen negative consequences following from his act, one may attempt to formulate the proscription of active scandal as follows: "You ought not to make a decision to perform or omit an act foreseen as resulting in the moral transgression of another." What follows from a strict observation of such a norm? In reply to this question it might be enlightening to take into account some related issues in Pauline writings. Although in his letter to the Romans as well as to the Corinthians Paul advises the Jewish Christians who are already mature in the faith to refrain from scandalizing the Gentile neophites by eating things sacrificed to idols (an act morally unobjectionable), he is not of the view that one should

----

4 cf. S. Th., II-II, q. 43, a. 1.

5 Some moralists teach that apart from offending against charity, a giver of scandal also sins against the virtue or commandment he incites his victim to violate. Thus to persuade another person, for instance, to commit an act of theft would be for the scandal-giver a sin against charity and against justice.

refrain from every act foreseen to result in "scandalum pusillorum". This is clear from the incident narrated in the letter to the Galatians chapter 2, 11-14.

During Peter's sojourn in Antioch he freely ate and drank with uncircumcised Gentiles until the arrival of some Jewish emissaries from James, who insisted on circumcision. The presence of the party places Peter in a dilemma. He had either to continue his association with the uncircumcised Gentiles or to dissociate himself from the group. The first alternative entails a practical proclamation of the true gospel, which in this case is that faith in Christ and not fidelity to the law leads to salvation. This alternative preserves the unity of the Church in Antioch but at the same time provides an occasion of scandal for the party from James. The second alternative is a silent denial of the gospel truth. This option removes the occasion of sin for the emissaries from James but threatens the unity of the Church of Antioch. Peter chooses the former alternative ostensibly to ensure that "scandalum pusillorum" does not result from his action. His choice attracts Paul's rebuke: "When I saw they were not respecting the true meaning of the Good News, I said to Cephas in front of everyone 'In spite of being a Jew, you live like the pagans and not like the Jews, so you have no right to make the pagans copy jewish ways'" (Gal. 2:14). Were the proscription of scandal formulated above to be followed strictly, Paul's reproach would be hardly justifiable. Similarly, actions which are morally unobjectionable from the dictates of moral common sense will be considered morally wrong if the proscription were to apply strictly. It would have been morally wrong for Christ to have taken the decision to carry out his saving mission since it was foreseen that it would provoke the Jews to laying violent hands on the Anointed One. It will also be morally wrong to advise or ask for the lesser of two evils. Furthermore, it will be morally wrong for police officers to leave marked money about in order to detect a thief who has proved a menace to a society, since that will provide the thief with another occasion of sin. This looks absurd!

It is thus clear that if the proscription of active scandal were to extend as wide as the above prohibition of scandal, then many actions usually considered by moralists as morally right or even mandatory will be classified as morally wrong. It is, nevertheless, a received teaching that the sinful consequences of an act cannot be excluded from the responsibility of the one who performs the act. Sin is a moral disvalue and by definition ought to be avoided at all costs. To avoid sin at all costs considered radically, would be taken to mean to desire that sin does not come into existence (6). But such a desire will remain ineffectual excepting that one is prepared to take a decision to do or omit every act foreseen to result in sin; whether in one's sin or in that of another person. This leads us back to our point of departure, namely, to the unacceptable far-stretching prohibition of acts foreseen to result in the sin of another person.

As a means of solving this dilemma, catholic moralists introduce the distinction between intending and permitting sin, that is to say,

----

6 cf. B. Schüller, **Die Begründung**, p. 185.

between direct scandal and indirect scandal. It is self evident that one may never intend sin directly since it is an absolute disvalue. "Voluntas volendo malum fit mala". One may, on the other hand, permit or tolerate sin as a foreseen by-product of something directly willed, if there is a proportionate reason. Thus one may advise the lesser of two evils in order to lessen the non-moral evil effects of the sin of the other and thereby permit the sin of the other foreseen to follow from the advice. Police officers intending to protect society from future menaces may leave marked notes about to detect a thief and permit the foreseen theft of the culprit.

It is obvious that in the face of sin, an absolute disvalue, the moral relevance of the distinction between intending and permitting evil is clear. But what does permitting sin by a human being mean? The answer to this question depends largely on what one takes "permit" to mean. Lexically, "to permit" means (a) "to allow" as the word is usually employed when one says: My Superior permits (allows) me to leave the community; or (b) "to admit of" as used in the following sentence: The situation does not permit (admit of) any delay. Of the above lexical meanings of "permit", "to allow" seems closer to its meaning as is used in the question above. A Superior allows or permits his subordinate to do something because he has the power to do so. A doctor is said to allow an incurable patient under his care to die because it is believed that he could prevent his death, that is to say, he could prolong the patient's life by the use of respirators.

Can it be meaningfully said that somebody allowed the sun to shine? No, because that the sun shines or not does not fall within the boundaries of what a human being can do. It seems therefore that it is only meaningful to use the word "allow" or "permit" in circumstances where one has the ability to allow or to permit as well as the ability to disallow or to prevent.

In a parallel manner it may be asked: Could one be said to prevent the sin of the other? It might seem that in circumstances similar to that in which a theft occurs because a police officer leaves marked notes about, it could be said that he could have prevented the theft had he not left the marked notes about. But what is the moral cause of the sin: his leaving the marked notes about or the free decision of the thief to remove the notes. Although the leaving of marked notes about provides the occasion for the other to commit the sin of the theft, it cannot be described as its moral cause. Even if the Police officer wills that the thief removes the notes, it cannot be strictly said that he was able to cause the act of theft. It is the sinner alone that can allow his sin to occur. To say that one allows the sin of the other is to stretch the meaning of the word "allow" wider than its common usage would permit. Moreover, it implies in a way, the suppression of the other's freedom of decision. Only God, as Prima Causa of all things that exist, can strictly be said to allow the sin of the other inasmuch as he chose to create a being capable of free choice and free self-determination.

It is thus evident the sin of the other, insofar as it has its cause in the free decision of the sinner to commit a morally wrong act, does not strictly speaking, result as an effect of the act of the giver of scandal which consists in the non-moral evil of providing the

the occasion of sin for the other. This non-moral evil effect could be directly intended when there is a proportionate reason. A Police officer may directly will to place marked notes about – an act which provides an occasion of sin – in order to detect a menacing thief.

Thus the moral permissibility of indirect scandal does not rest in the fact that the evil effect of the action (scandal-giving) was not intended. The effect of the action of a giver of scandal, strictly speaking, is not the sin of the other but the occasion of this sin, which is a non-moral evil. One can not sincerely say that a police officer, who secretly leaves marked notes in order to trace a menacing thief, does not will that the thief takes the notes. If removing these notes is a necessary means (bonum utile) for identifying the thief and the police officer chose it, it cannot be reasonably said that he did not intend it.

3.1.2. COOPERATION IN THE SIN OF ANOTHER

One who makes a comparative study of the treatment giving by catholic moralists to cooperation in the sin of another in their various manuals can hardly fail to recall the well known saying that England and America are two countries separated by the same language. It is not seldom that these moralists use some of the technical terms usually employed within this context without defining them in a clear manner (7). The result is that often they employ terms such as material and formal cooperation as homonyms and thereby create room for ambiguity and confusion. To clear this confusion it will prove rewarding at the beginning of the discussion of this topic, to have a clear view of what tradition takes cooperation in the sin of the other to mean, and how formal and material cooperation differ from each other.

3.1.2.1. Notion of cooperation

In a wide sense, cooperation is understood as participating in the sinful act of another person. The various ways by which one is

----

7 In his article, "Über die Mitwirkung zur Sünde des Nebenmenschen", in: Zeitschrift für Katholische **Theologie**, 3 (1879) 494-495, Noldin identifies some of the problems entailed in the understanding of the traditional treatment of cooperation in the sin of another. He says: "Wie die Schwierigkeit des Gegenstandes anerkannt wird, so gesteht man auch ziemlich offen, daß alles, was bisher über dieses Kapitel geschrieben wurde, nicht recht befriedigt. In der Tat sind die hierher gehörigen Begriffe nicht genau bestimmt und oft mißverständlich, die Prinzipien unklar, die Anwendungen desselben schwankend und die Lösung der einzelnen Fragen und Gewissensfälle zweifelhaft und widersprechend."

considered a participator in the sin of another are summarised in the well-known verse: iussio, concilium, consensus, palpa, recursus, participans, mutus, non-obstans, non manifestans (8). Thus cooperation understood in the wide sense embraces positive acts like commanding, advising, urging and flattering somebody to sin. It also includes negative acts like not hindering or manifesting a malefactor by which a person silently encourages another in the doing of moral evil. Cooperation understood in this sense is a sort of "causa peccati". Here a person does not necessarily help in the physical execution of the sinful act.

It could happen, on the other hand, that a person takes a free and independent decision to perform a sinful act and later seeks the corporal assistance of another in order to execute his sinful design. Rendering concrete aid to such a person is known as cooperation in the strict sense. Noldin and Schmitt describe it as "concursus physicus ad pravam actionem alterius principaliter agentis" (9). It is in this sense that moral theologians use the word when they talk of cooperation in the sin of another.

It is not seldom that cooperation is confused with scandal. Although both are closely related they are two distinct and different realities. In what does their difference lie? In replying to this question it is worthwhile to keep in mind that in the deliberate performance of a morally wrong act, there are two moments: the internal decision to perform the act, and the execution of the act itself. It is possible that a person exerts some influence on the will of the other by providing the occasion of sin or even by willing that his neighbour takes a decision to carry out a morally wrong act without himself assisting in the concrete execution of the immoral act. It is also possible that somebody may assist another already decided in performing a morally depraved act in the execution of his decision.

The instance, where the decision to sin arises from some external influence, is a case of scandal. Here a man's act (word or omission) as it were 'causes' (10), the sin of the other. In contrast, in cooperation "in sensu stricto", the other, who is assisted, has already taken an independent decision to sin. The execution of the sinful design depends on the cooperator: a) completely, insofar as there are sins that cannot be committed without foreign assistance (cooperatio necessarius) or b) partially, insofar as the principal agent can execute his sinful plans (perhaps with more difficulties) without external assistance (cooperatio non-necessarius).

Briefly stated cooperation "in sensu stricto" presupposes the decision of the other to sin while scandal presumes, on the other hand, that the other's will was good or at least indifferent to the sin in question. While scandal is describable as "causa occasionalis interni

----

8 cf. S. Th. II-II, q. 62, a. 7.

9 H. Noldin and A. Schmitt, op. cit., vol. 2, p. 116.

10 Here "cause" is to be understood as "causa occasionalis vel alliciens". The formal cause of sin can only be found in the bad will of the other.

peccati" in regard to the sin of the scandalized, cooperation could be said to be a sort of "causa externi peccati" with regard to the sin (morally wrong act) of the principal agent.

3.1.2.2. Formal and material cooperation

It is true that the principal agent by freely and independently deciding to perform an act he knows to be morally wrong has sinned already and that the external act does not have a different morality from the internal. Nevertheless, by executing the sinful act the internal sin, when not repeated or multiplied, is at least increased intensively. The guilt of executing a sinful design may increase particularly when damage is done to a third party. One, who takes a decision to kill his fellow man as a means of taking revenge has sinned in his heart, that is to say, he has committed a morally bad act. By executing this sinful design, he commits a morally wrong act. Now the duty of love impels a man not only to do good to his neighbour but also, as far as possible, to prevent evil from befalling him. Just as this duty demands that he averts material evil from his fellow men, it also obliges him to hinder spiritual harm from befalling them. Thus this duty forbids him to cooperate in bringing a spiritual or material harm to a fellow man. Accordingly, cooperating with another in the execution of a sinful act is evidently a failure in one's moral obligation.

One may attempt to formulate the prohibition of cooperation in the sin of another in the following way: "You may not perform an act foreseen to be misused by another person to his spiritual harm". If this norm prohibiting cooperation were to be observed strictly, exactly the same problems that arise from the prohibition of every act foreseen to occasion passive scandal will come into existence. Thus many acts usually deemed by moralists as morally right or even mandatory will be classified as morally wrong. An example will help to add more light to this fact.

A highway man orders a servant to surrender his master's wallet or be shot. If the servant surrenders the wallet, he cooperates in act of robbery. If he fails to surrender it, he cooperates in the act of murder. Thus if the strict prohibition of every act of cooperation were to be followed the servant performs a morally wrong act whether or not he complies to the order of the highway man. This is absurd since no conflict situation can leave a man with options which are all morally wrong.

However, if the servant decides to surrender the wallet or his life he cannot distance himself from the negative consequences, loss of property or loss of life, following his decision – a decision which has the consequences of assisting the highway man execute his sinful design.

The way catholic tradition tries to steer its way out of this dilemma is well known. It distinguishes between formal (direct) and material (indirect) cooperation (11). Formal cooperation is always prohibited while material cooperation may be permitted for a proportionate reason.

What does the terms formal and material cooperation designate? To understand these terms, it may be worthwhile to trace their genesis into catholic moral tradition. One of the issues that generated much controversy among moral theologians in the 17th and 18th centuries was the problem of probabilism. At both extremes of this controversy were rigorists and laxists respectively. To check some of the aberrations resulting from these debates, the Holy Office intervened in 1679 with the condemnation of sixty-five propositions. One of the condemned propositions reads:

> "Famulus, qui submissis humeris, scienter adjuvat herum suum ascendere per fenestram ad stuprandam virginem et multoties eidem subservit deferendo scalam, aperiendo januam, aut quid simile cooperando, non peccat mortaliter, si id metu notabilis detrimenti, puta, ne a domino male tractetur, ne torvis oculis aspiciatur, ne domo expellatur" (DS 2151).

The exact meaning of this condemnation and the reason for it offered materials for discussions among moralists. Their debate spinned around the questions whether the servant's act is condemned because it is deemed an intrinsic (moral) evil whose performance in every circumstance is prohibited or whether it is condemned because a proportionate reason is lacking to justify it in this case? Some theologians proposed the view that it was condemned because a proportionate reason was lacking. Others stood in the opposite camp and argued that it was condemned because the act was intrinsically (moral) evil (12). St. Alphonsus for instance, in the first edition of his manual, which is simply a commentary on the text of Hermann Busembaum, propounds the view that the act is intrinsically evil (13).

----

11 It is important to note that authors are not generally agreed on what "principium divisionis" to employ when making the distinction between formal and material cooperation. An author may classify an act under implicit formal cooperation and insist that it is always sinful while another may group the same act under immediate material cooperation and maintain that although it is sinful in most instances there are exceptions possible. For concrete illustration of this point cf. Henry Peschke, op. cit., vol. 1, pp. 251-252.

12 cf. Roger Roy, "La cooperation selon Saint Alphonse de Liguori", Studia Moralia, VI (1968), p. 415-421.

13 Alphonsus Maria de Ligorio, **Medulla Theologia Moralis R.P. Hermani Busembaum societatis Jesu** Theologi cum Adnotationibus, (Nicapolii 1748), 1.2, t. 3, c. 2, d. 5, a. 3, nn. 61 ff.

However, in later editions (14), Alphonsus changes his opinion and argues that the act is not intrinsically evil. He maintains that the crime of ravaging a virgin is so monstrous that only a grave reason such as fear of death could justify cooperating in an instance of its type. Alphonsus distinguishes between formal and material cooperation. Formal cooperation consists in concurring with the bad will of the other, while material cooperation consists in concurring or participating in the morally wrong action of the other (15).

Whether a cooperator renders a "cooperatio necessarius" or a "cooperatio non-necessarius" in the execution of a sinful plan, two things are possible in so far as his cooperation relates to the internal sinful decision of the principal agent. Either he approves of the sinful decision of the principal agent or he does not. If the cooperator, knowing that such a decision is morally wrong and inspite of his knowledge approves of it, his cooperation is described as "cooperatio formalis". A cooperation is called "formal" whether a cooperator explicitly approves of the sinful decision of the other as in the case of one who encourages or urges the principal agent to carry out the sinful decision or whether the cooperator does not expressly approve of the sinful decision of the other as in the case of one who silently wants the other to sin. Whether a cooperator's assistance consists in carrying out an act intrinsically evil or indifferent, he cooperates formally if he freely approves of the sinful decision of the principal agent, which he knows to be morally wrong.

If a cooperator does not approve of the sinful decision of the other and for some reason participates in the execution of the other's sinful decision, that is to say, in the execution of a morally wrong act, his cooperation is known as "material cooperation". The cooperator in this case performs an act with a motive different from the sinful plan

----

14 Alphonsus Maria de Ligorio, **Theologia Moralis,** ed. Leonardus Gaude, (Romae 1905), 1.2. t. 3, c. 2, d. 5, a. 3, nn. 61 ff.

15 Alphonsus, ibid, n. 63, asserts: "illam esse formalem, quae concurrit ad malam voluntatem alterius, et nequit esse sine peccato; materialem vero illam, quae concurrit tantum ad malam actionem alterius, praeter intentionem cooperantis."
One searches in vain for the definition of formal and material cooperation among the older moralists. They did not make the distinction. However, that is not to say that they were completely ignorant of the two realities. What is today known as formal cooperation was described by Sanchez (Opus morale in praec. decal., 1. 1, c. 1, n. 1) and Valentia (Comm. theol., tom. III, disp. 5, q. 21, p. 4) as direct cooperation. In his treatment of cooperation P. Laymann, uses the terms "material" and "formal" but does not define them. He says: Quare recte a quibusdam dicitur, nefas esse cooperari alterus peccato formaliter ut peccatum est; fas tamen esse interdum materialiter cooperari, quod peccatum est." (Theol. mor., 1.2, tr. 3, c. 13 n. 4).

or motive of the principal agent. The object of his act can (using traditional terminology) either be indifferent or intrinsically evil. While some authors (16) following St. Alphonsus, propound the view that the participation in an intrinsic evil act could be called material cooperation, if the sinful design of the other is not approved of, others (17) argue that each of such participation is ipso facto formal cooperation. For instance August Rohling (18) writes:

"cooperatio formalis duplex est:
a) Si actus cooperans per se indifferens ponatur cum intentione, ut alter peccatum peragere vel securius ad liberius peccare possit; nam directe velle peccatum semper est illicitum.
b) Si actus cooperans sit in se illicitus seu intrinsece malus."

As illustrations of intrinsic evil he cites lying, abortion in order to save the mother, perjury etc. As is evident, the examples he gives are dressed in value terms. Among other things each connotes a morally evil intention. For instance Rohling describes "medacium" as "locutio contra mentem cum intentione fallendi" (19).

If a man were to cooperate in an act of lying, so defined, he participates in the execution of falsehood. Since the intention to declare what is false belongs to the essence of lying as Rohling asserts (20), one cannot cooperate in the act of lying without approving of the intention of the principal agent. Thus Rohling's example of lying even reveals that in formal cooperation approval is always given to the principal agent's intention to perform a morally objectionable act.

The immoral character of formal cooperation is evident in its definition, namely, approving of a morally depraved act. A person who cooperates formally unites his will with the sinful will of the principal agent and thereby shares fully in the sin. This fact is brought into clear light by the teaching on restitution. Those who, acting out of solidarity of will, harm a third party are liable to making "restitutio in solidum". In primo loco, both are to pay full compensation.

---

16 Cretoni, one of the editors of the works of Gury is of this opinion and says that "cooperatio in hoc casu illicito sit qua actio, non qua cooperatio". See Stephinsky, Der Katholik, Mainz (1876), p. 350.

17 August Rohling, **Medulla theologiae moralis**, (St. Louis 1875), p. 66; Lehmkuhl) **Theologia moralis**, (Freiburg Herder 1888), n. 646.

18 Augustus Rohling, ibid., p. 66 ff.

19 Augustus Rohling, ibid., p. 249.

20 Augustus Rohling, ibid., p. 249.

In secundo loco, should one of the parties refuse to pay compensation, the other is obliged to compensate fully (21).

Sin is an absolute disvalue; one may never say "yes" to it. Thus asserting that formal cooperation is forbidden is analytic. It is evident that the distinction between direct (formal) and indirect (informal) cooperation is morally relevant in so far as it is a distinction between approving and not-approving of a morally wrong act.

Whether material assistance is rendered or not, the sin of the principal agent is not altered. Must cooperation be called material (indirect) in order to be permitted? To put the question in a different way: Is cooperation permitted because the execution of the sin of the principal agent – one of the effects of the act of cooperation – is not approved of? The example employed already may help to articulate this question.

A servant carrying the wallet of his master is ordered by a highway man to surrender either the wallet or his life. He surrenders the wallet. Is his surrendering the wallet morally right because he did not will or approve of the thief's sinful decision or simply because he had a proportionate reason to do so.

By asking him to choose between surrendering the wallet or his life, the highway man is, as it were, asking the servant to choose between two non-moral evils: the loss of some material property or the loss of a human life. By opting for the former, the servant chooses the lesser of two non-moral evils. Thus his choice is justified for a proportionate reason. The question of approving of and not approving of the sinful act of the other does not seem to come into play in the moral assessment of the act.

3.2. DIRECT/INDIRECT AS APPLICABLE TO ACTS DEONTOLOGICALLY APPRAISED

3.2.1. ACTS CONSIDERED MORALLY WRONG BECAUSE THEY ARE CONTRA NATURAM: THE USE OF ARTIFICIAL CONTRACEPTIVE DEVICES AND MASTURBATION

In treating the sins chastity or the offences contrary to the sixth commandment, catholic manuals of moral theology usually distinguish

----

21 cf. Mausbach-Ermecke, op. cit., vol. 3, p.562. In contrast, those, who acting out of different motives, simultaneously and co-jointly harm a third party are only liable to "restitutio pro rata"; each has only to pay for the amount of harm he caused.

between "peccati secundum naturam" (1): fornication, adultery, incest, rape, sacrilege and "peccati contra naturam": sodomy, bestiality, masturbation (self-pollution or ipsation) and the use of contraceptive devices. Among the sins described as contrary to nature two are relevant to the problem under consideration here. These include masturbation and the use of artificial contraceptive devices. What role does the direct/indirect distinction play in the moral assessment of these acts?

The teaching on birth regulation states that responsible parenthood means more than a generous generation of children. It also implies the limitation of the number of children as is required by the circumstances in which the married couples find themselves. Physical, psychological and social conditions can make it imperative for a married couple to have no children for a period of time or even for an indefinite period. If, for instance, another pregnancy will be detrimental to the health of a married woman or if one more child in the family will hinder a married couple from providing adequately for the existing children, it is the duty of the couple, as responsible parents, to prevent further conception.

In a situation of this type, the teaching on birth regulation does not require that the married couples refrain completely from having marital relations. It rather demands that they restrict their marital acts to the safe-period, that is to say, they could use the rhythm method of birth regulation. While they are permitted to use this method, they are forbidden to use artificial means like the pill, condom, spermicidal jellies, diaphragm, or intrauterine devices. Why are these artificial means of birth control said to be illegal?

In replying to this question Catholic tradition takes recourse to the nature or finality of sexual organs. Since God as a rational being does not act arbitrarily, he has some purpose for creating each organ of the body. The eye, for instance, is made for the purpose of sight; the ear for hearing and the sexual organs (primarily) for generating of offspring. Some problems arise when the ends of organs that have more than one function are considered. The tongue, for example, serves different ends: talking, tasting and eating. Similarly, the sexual organs serve different purposes: procreation of offspring and fostering of mutual love between married couples. It may then be asked: for which of these purposes did God equip man with the sexual organs?

Catholic tradition replies to this question by declaring that God, in creating these organs, intends that they be used primarily for the procreating of offspring. It may be argued that if according to God's will the procreation of children is the primary end of the marital act, it might seem that performing such an act with a sterile partner or

----

1   From the fact that Tradition talks of "peccati secundum naturam" one deduces immediately that "nature" in this context is not identifiable with the natural (moral) law. One also sees that the "principium divisionis" employed in grouping sins into "secundum naturam" and "contra naturam" is not on the basis of what corresponds to the natural (moral) law and what does not.

with a spouse expecting a baby, or with one in her safe-period will be contravening God's will, since in these instances the material act is not productive of offspring. It will then be immoral to have sexual relations with a spouse in any of these conditions. Catholic tradition tries to obviate this problem by teaching that as long as the fruitfulness of the marital act is not impaired by human intervention the act is not contrary to God's will. In contrast, by deliberately making the marital act unfruitful by some artificial intervention, one acts contrary to nature, one vitiates the eternal plan of the Omniscient Creator. Arguing in this manner Tradition concludes that the use of artificial means of preventing conception is illegal.

Exactly the same argument is employed by Catholic tradition in the moral evaluation of masturbation. Sketching the traditional argument for the proscription of masturbation, C. Henry Peschke asserts:

> "The inner reason for the defectiveness and disorder of masturbation lies in this that the sexual power is used in a way not intended by the Creator. The basic purpose of sexual activity is the procreation of offspring and the expression as well as fostering of mutual love between husband and wife ... This double end of sexual activity is frustrated in the solitary practice of masturbation; the true, proper meaning of sexual activity is not realised." (23)

Thus masturbation, just as the use of artificial contraceptive devices, is said to be illicit because it vitiates the finality set by the Omniscient God in creating the sexual organs. Reasoning in this way, catholic tradition proscribes masturbation as well as the use of artificial contraceptive devices as morally wrong irrespective of their good results or the intention of the agent.

Since the use of artificial methods of birth control as well as deliberate self-pollution are generally considered sinful by tradition, one may attempt to formulate the deontological norm prohibiting such acts respectively as follows:

a) "You may not take a decision to perform an act foreseen to frustrate the sexual act."

b) "You may not take a decision to perform an act foreseen to lead to self-pollution."

If these prohibitions were to be observed strictly, certain actions generally accepted by moralists to be morally unobjectionable will be considered morally wrong. For instance, it will be morally wrong for a surgeon to perform an operation he foresees will result in his polluting himself. In such a situation, it would seem that his moral duty would consist in letting the patient die. Similarly, it will also be considered morally wrong for a married woman, whose irregular menstrual cycle is menacing to her hygiene, to take progesteron com-

---

23 C. Henry Peschke, **Christian Ethics** (Alcester and Dublin 1978), vol. 2, p. 403-404.

pounds to normalize it, if she foresees that such will frustrate the fruitful effects of the marital act.

In contrast to indirect self-pollution and indirect use of artificial method of preventing pregnancy, direct self-pollution and direct use of artificial method of preventing pregnancy, are considered always illegal. No reason is grave enough to permit such acts. A couple whose much desired objective of having a child is realizable only by means of the so called homologous insemination act illegally if they intend to obtain the sperm needed for this procedure by means of masturbation. Similarly, couples who wish to test their fertility act morally wrong if they intend to obtain the sperm necessary for the procedure by means of ipsation. Although a couple may rightly decide to avoid having more children in the future in order to be able to provide adequately for the existing ones, it is nevertheless deemed forbidden for the wife to strive to attain this objective by taking contraceptive pills. These acts are all considered illegal. Much as they are never to be performed because they are contrary to nature, they are also never to be intended.

This argument which considers an act morally wrong because it is contrary to nature or to God's will was widely used in the past. Schüller (24) points out that Epitectus maintains that a man should not shave his beard because God in his wisdom intends to distinguish between man and woman and so wills that the former wears a beard. In addition he shows that Tertullian argues against the use of cosmetics because those who apply such are not satisfied with God's product. They reproach God by trying to improve on his work. Similarly, Michael Offiong (25) notes that Caesar of Arles considers illicit the use of portion to fecundate a sterile woman because in his eyes this meant a violation of the state of affairs as willed by God. He also points out that during the reign of Philip II of Spain (1527-98) a commission rejected a project aimed at rendering Rivers Tagus and Manazanaros in Spain navigable because the members believed that if God had wished that these rivers be navigable, he would have made them so with a word. Furthermore, he shows that around the same period, moralists of note declared illicit any irrigative operations.

APPRECIATION OF THE "CONTRARY TO GOD'S WILL" OR
"CONTRARY TO NATURE" ARGUMENT

Just as the bible, creation is sometimes considered a book of Revelation. God's will is said to be manifested both in the bible and in the work of creation. For the sake of argument it will be assumed that God's will as manifested in the bible and in the works of crea-

----

24 Bruno Schüller, **Die Begründung sittlicher Urteile**, pp. 216-217.

25 Michael Offiong, Unpublished notes on "Desacralization of creation", (Enugu Nigeria 1976), p. 4.

tion is equivalent to the moral law. From this it follows that what God commands is morally right and what He forbids is morally wrong. If this relationship between God's will and the morally right or the morally wrong were to be considered, a well-known dilemma which is found in Plato's Euthyphro (26) arises. Is performing a given action right (wrong) because God wills us to do (refrain from doing) it; or God wills that we perform (refrain from doing) it because it is right (wrong)? Accepting the first horn of this dilemma amounts to propounding a theistic moral positivism. Morality is founded upon a free divine choice. A morally evil act will be morally right if only God commands it. Abraham's attempt to use Isaac, his only son, as a sacrifice to Yahwe (Gen. 22:1-19), Hosea's marriage to a whore (Hos. 1:2), the plundering of the property of the Egyptians – clothing silver ornaments and gold – by the Israelites (Ex. 12:35), are morally right because God commanded them (27). Evidently, Catholic tradition does not propound this indefensible ethical opinion.

In contrast, Catholic tradition expouses the second horn of the dilemma. God is thought of as the Good Father who wills only that which is good and right for his children. The fact that God commands an act is a guarantee that it is morally right and that He forbids an act is an unmistakable evidence of its moral objectionable character. From the foregoing, it is clear that God's will is synonymous with the morally right. Therefore, a moral argument which asserts that an act is morally right because it accords with God's will or an act is morally wrong because it is contrary to God's will is question begging. It simply asserts in different words that an act is morally right because it is morally right or an act is morally wrong because it is morally wrong. The question: Why is masturbation or the use of artificial means of birth control wrong seeks the reason why it is forbidden by God, that is to say, why it is morally wrong. Accordingly, the answer to this question cannot be: because it is forbidden by God. God does not act arbitrarily. As a rational being, He always prescribes or proscribes acts with some reason.

---

26 Plato, **Euthypro**, 9 e.

27 Exegetes do not take these texts literally. The first is seen as the test of Abraham's faith. The fathers saw it as prefiguring the passion of Jesus, the only begotten Son. The Second is seen as symbolically representing Yahwe's marriage with Israel. Inspite of Israel's repeated acts of flirtation with alien God's, Yahweh still loves this faithless people and cherishes them when they repent. The third, the willingness of the Egyptians to provide gold, silver and clothing is explained to match the Egyptian mentality: God has proved his strength, to allow his people to leave empty handed is an affront. Cf. the corresponding commentaries in the **Jerusalem Bible** and **The Jerome Biblical Commentary**, ed. R.E. Brown, (N.Y. Englewood Cliffs 1974).

One other logical error that often pervades the arguments that deems an act wrong because it is contrary to God's will or nature, as Schüller (28) observes is the fallacy of equivocation. This is because words like 'God's will' and 'natural law' are used to designate realities other than the morally right. God's will could stand for God's Providence. In this sense whatever happens or whatever is the case is said to be the will of the Creator who is "Causa Prima". Thus that a man dies prematurely, inspite of every medical care; that a marital act is fruitless inspite of the strong wish of a couple to have a child, are God's will. 'Natural law' can also designate physical, biological or psychological law in so far as God as "Causa Prima" is operative through secondary causes. That two atoms of hydrogen combine with one atom of oxygen to produce water, that progesteron compounds make a marital act fruitless, that the marital act of two non-sterile couples results in the procreation of offspring are in accord with the law of nature.

Failure to distinguish 'natural law' as designating the moral law, on the other hand, and physical, biological or psychological law, on the other, has led Catholic tradition to arguing that contravening the latter tantamounts to offending against the former (29). This error explains why it concludes that masturbation and the use of contraceptive devices are moral evils. Masturbation and the use of contraceptives in so far as they are contrary to the natural law understood in the second sense can be nothing else other than the causing of non-moral evils (30). If they are to be seen as the production of non-moral evils, nothing hinders one to intend such acts as a means when there is a proportionate grave reason to perform them. Thus the distinction between direct/indirect in so far as it applies to masturbation and the use of contraceptives does not play a morally significant role. Direct masturbation, for instance, simply designates self-pollution performed without proportionate reason. Similarly direct use of artificial contraceptive device signifies the using of such a device without a proportionate grave reason.

----

28 Bruno Schüller, **Die Begründung sittlicher Urteile**, p. 235.

29 Bruno Schüller, ibid., p. 232, points out that both senses are employed in the Encyclical Letter, **Humanae Vitae**, n. 11.

30 It is instructive to note that statements made by certain Episcopal Conferences on the **Humanae Vitae** shows that they take the use of contraceptive as a non-moral evil justifiable for a proportionate reason. For instance, the Swiss Episcopal Conference is of the opinion that spouses of goodwill, who see no other reasonable solution for their problems than to use contraceptives, are in this case not guilty of sin. "If, in a special case, they are not able to meet all the norms of the encyclical concerning birth control, and as long as they do not in any way act out of egoism, but rather in all sincerity strive to fulfill the divine will always better, they can lawfully judge that in their case they are not guilty before God." cf. Edwardus Hamel: Conferentiae Episcopales et Encyclica Humanae Vitae", Periodica, 58 (1969), p. 234-439.

3.2.2. ACTS WRONG BECAUSE THEY ARE PERFORMED "EX DEFECTU JURIS IN AGENTE":

KILLING OF AN INNOCENT PERSON AND MUTILATION

The Holy Writ expressly proscribes the killing of an innocent person. Exodus 23,7 declares: "See that the man who is innocent is not done to death"; and Daniel 13,53 demands: "You must not put the innocent and the just to death". Catholic tradition understands this proscription of the killing of an innocent person as a deontoligical norm. Thomas Aquinas (31), for instance, teaches that it is never lawful even for a public authority to kill an innocent person no matter what benefit may accure to the community from his death. Manuals of moral theology under the influence of Thomas teach that under no circumstance may a man directly kill an innocent person, not even when such an act may save other 100 people (32). Pius XI wonders whether any reason could ever justify the direct killing of an innocent person (33).

A statement like "It is wrong to kill an innocent person" is synthetic. One does not immediately see why one ought not. In attempting to offer the reason Catholic tradition argues that killing an innocent person is wrong because it is an act performed "ex defectu juris in agente". By killing an innocent person a man acts beyond his powers and arrogates to himself the power of God. God as the Creator is Lord of life and death (Dt. 32,39). He alone as the Almighty Maker has, as it were, the right of dominion over human life (34). He can dispose of human life as he chooses. His right over human life excludes human beings from possessing such a right. Accordingly a man has no right to dispose of himself as he chooses.

The same argument is employed by tradition in justifying her deontological prohibition of mutilation. Man, as care-taker, has no right

----

31 S. Th., II-II, q. 64, a. 6.

32 Dominic Prümmer preserves the tone tradition employs in her prohibition of direct killing when he says! "Unter keinen Umständen darf man einen Menschen direkt töten, wenn man auch hundert andere Leben dadurch retten könnte." cf. D. Prümmer, "Medizinische Eingriffe in das keimende Leben, betrachtet vom Standpunkt der katholischen Moral", Linzer Quartalsschrift, 74 (1921), pp. 565-570.

33 AAS, 22 (1930): p. 563.

34 A similar view is discernable in the writings of Plato. In **Phaedo** 62c we read: "If one of your possessions were to destroy itself without intimation from you that you wanted it to die, wouldn't you be angry with it and punish it, if you had any means of doing so ... So if you look at it in this way I suppose it is not unreasonable to say that we must not put an end to ourselves until God sends some compulsion."

to dispose of the members of his body. Only God enjoys this special prerogative.

Does this argument provide a compelling reason for the moral objectionable nature of mutilation and the killing of an innocent person? Are these acts, when considered in themselves to be seen as the causing of moral evils or of non-moral evils? The last question will be considered first.

The teaching of Catholic tradition on transplantation of organs provides a good illustration of the problems contained in the question.

TRANSPLANTATION OF ORGANS

The transplantation of organs involves two major medical procedures which have some relevance to ethics.

1) The removal of the organ from the donor and,

2) The implantation of this organ in the recipient.

The second procedure, which does not directly concern the problem at issue here, touches ethical questions such as: Is the surgical operation undertaken with the consent of the patient? Or where he is unable to give consent by reason of age or ill-health, is there a vicarious consent given by a competent relation? Is there some proportion between the risk involved in the operation and the chances of its being a success?

The first procedure, which is relevant to the question being dealt here, presents minor problems if the donor is dead. In this case, only the question whether the deceased or his competent relation consented to the procedure. However, when homologous transplantation is "inter vivos", some vexing questions emerge. May a man donate a kidney, for instance, in order to help save the life of an ailing neighbour? Is it ever permitted for a man, a care-taker, to mutilate any of his members?

Catholic tradition usually replies to the last question by having recourse to the principle of totality, a principle permeated with teleological logic. It states that since the members of the body exist for the good of the whole body, one may lawfully sacrifice a disaesed or healthy member which threatens the welfare of the whole. A rigid application of the principle of totality would exclude from the realm of morally right acts like the submission to interventions such as experimentation (35) and caesarian operation for the sake of a foetus as well as the donation of organs for transplantation.

In treating the problem of the donation of organs for transplantation, catholic moralists of the past generally distinguish between the donation of blood and skin and the donation of major organs like kidney, liver and lungs. The former is not considered a difficult problem. In spite of the prescription of the principle of totality some theologians argue that since blood and skin naturally restore themselves easily, that is to say, since the harm done is temporary, one may legitimately donate such organs (36). It is the moral rightness of the donation of the major organs that divides theological opinion. While competent moralists like Mausbach-Ermecke (37) and M. Zalba (38) argue that it is always illicit, other respectable moralists like Gerard Kelly (39) and Thomas J. O. Donnell (40) maintain that it is permissible under certain conditions. What arguments do they employ to back their stand?

The argument employed by some of these theologians in justifying the donation of major organs for transplantation is similar to that Arthur Vermeersch uses in supporting the donation of blood and skin Vermeersch's argument runs as follows:

The unity of the human race by which we are in certain manner one with the neighbour can perhaps also explain why someone may directly cause some injury on his body for the welfare of his neighbour. Such is the case when someone, for instance, offers a piece of his skin so that the wound of his neighbour may be healed or when someone donates blood so that another person may live by it. Should we

---

35 Pius XII (AAS, 44 (1952), p. 788), saw the necessity of some human experimentation. To avoid risks altogether will be beyond human capabilities and in fact will paralyze research. Similarly, many eminent moralists like J. Ford, "Notes on Moral Theology", Theological Studies 6 (1945), p. 563 and G. Kelly, "Pope Pius XII and the Principle of Totality", Theological Studies 16 (1955), p. 383, believe that within certain limits human experimentation is permissible.

36 cf. Mausbach-Ermecke, op. cit., vo. 3, p. 254. How compelling is this argument employed in justifying the donation of minor organs? It appears that it did not occur to the theologians of that age that following this argument one could assert: sterilization as a contraceptive device is prohibited because the damage done is definitive and irreparable, while the use of contraceptive pills is permitted because its sterilizing effect is temporary.

37 Mausbach-Ermecke, ibid., p. 253.

38 M. Zalba, **Theologiae Moralis Compendium**, 1 (BAC 175),1958,nr.1576.

39 Gerard Kelly, **Medico-Moral Problems**, Dublin Clonmore and Reynolds 1960, p. 246.

40 Thomas J. O. Donnell, **Morals in Medicine**, Westminster Md Newman press 1962, pp. 266-268.

not suppose that our corporal organs are destined in a certain manner for the body of our neighbour (41)?

It is remarkable to note that reasoning this way, Vermeersch presents the finality of the human organs in a way different from its understanding in the formulation of the principle of totality (42). Secondly, he tries to widen the scope of the principle of totality and thus understands "body" as the human race.

Pius XII does not believe that the principle of totality can be reasonably extended to justify homologous transplant of organs. He says:

> "In this instance the members of the individual would be considered as parts, and members of the whole organism which constitutes 'humanity', in the same manner – or almost in the same manner – as they are parts of the individual organism of man. Then it is argued that, if it is permitted, when necessary, to sacrifice a particular member (hand, foot, eye, ear, kidney, sexual gland) to the organism of man, it should likewise be permitted to sacrifice a particular member to the organism "humanity" (in the person of one of its members who is sick and suffering). The purpose visualised by this manner of argumentation, to heal, or at least to soothe the ailments of others, is understandable and praiseworthy, but the method proposed and the argument on which it is based are erroneous." (43)

Bearing the position of the Pontiff in mind, some theologians who believe that the donation of organs for transplantation is morally justifiable, argue that, although the principle of totality cannot be used in supporting the moral permissibility of organ donation, the

----

41 A. Vermeersch, **Theologiae Moralis**, Romae 3 ed. 1945, vol. 2, p. 288.

42 It is worthy of note that Pius XII has a different opinion regarding the finality of the organs of the body. In his view the organs of the body are destined for the welfare of the possessor. He asserts: "The physical organism of living beings, plants, animals, and man have a unity existing on its own: each of the members, for example, the hand, the foot, the heart, the eye is an integral part, destined in its whole being to be inserted into the totality of the organism. Outside the organism, on account of its very nature, it possesses no meaning, no finality; it is entirely absorbed by the totality of the organism to which it is tied". AAS, 44 (1952), p. 786. See also AAS, 48 (1956), p. 46.

43 Pius XII, "Speech to the Italian Association of Blood Donors, March 8 1959', The Pope Speaks, vol. 5, nr. 3, (Summer 1959), p. 334.

principle does not forbid it (44). One of such theologians is Gerard Kelly who approves of the transplantation or organs. He says:

> "Organic transplantation is licit, provided that it confers a proportionate benefit on the recipient, without exposing the donor to great risk of life, or depriving him completely of an important function. The principal argument for the opinion is the law of charity, which is based on the natural and supernatural unity of mankind and according to which one's neighbour is another's self." (45)

Kelly seems to have taken the moral rightness of excising an organ for transplantation for self-evident and thus devotes no more effort to justifying the procedure. Naturally those who argue against the procedure would observe that he has missed the point. In their eyes he would look like one who made a good journey but unfortunately did so in the wrong train. The question asked concerns the moral rightness of excising organs for the purpose of transplantation. The reply given by Kelly is that the motive of the procedure is morally good.

One thing is evident in the arguments of all who justify mutilation for the purpose of transplantation. They do not deem the act of mutilating as the causing of a moral disvalue. In their opinion, it is evidently the causing of a non-moral disvalue whose causation is justifiable for a proportionate reason.

In contrast, those who argue against the transplantation of the major organs, judge the procedure as morally wrong. For instance, Mausbach-Ermecke (46) in discussing the problem demands that one must distinguish between the motive of the donor, on the one hand, and the object of the act of transplantation, on the other. If the object of the act is morally wrong no good or praiseworthy motive like love of neighbour can transform the morally evil character of the act. Mausbach-Ermecke further maintain that the removal of organs has a "moralitas interna conditionata". It is only allowed when the requirements of the principle of totality are met with. If the demands of the

----

44 Observing that moralists approve of a mother undergoing a caesarean section for the benefit of her unborn child – a directly intended major mutilation for the benefit of another – John R. Connery, "Notes on Moral Theology", Theological Studies 17 (1956), pp. 559-561, remarks: "It is precisely to the principle of charity that moralists appeal in justifying it, and no attempt is made to reconcile it with the principle of totality. Considering this fact with those mentioned above, I would include that while the principle of totality could never be used to justify transplantation, neither does it clearly exclude it."

45 G. Kelly, 'Pope Pius XII and the Principle of Totality', Th. St., 16 (1955), pp. 373-396. See also **Directive 30 of the Ethical and Religious Directive for Catholic Health Facilities** (Nov. 1971).

46 Mausbach-Ermecke, op. cit., vol. 3, 252-253.

principle are not attained the procedure is always prohibited as the performance of an act "propter defectum iuris in agente". Since a man has only the right of administration over the members and organs of his body (47), he may not dispose any of them as he wished. None, as it were, may make a gift of something over which he has no right of ownership.

From the foregoing it is clear that the disputing parties disagree basically on whether to classify the procedure of excising a body-member for the purpose of organ transplantation as the causing of a non-moral or a moral evil. While those who permit the procedure deem it the causation of a non-moral evil justifiable for a proportionate reason, those opposed to it qualify it as the causing of a moral evil because it is an act performed "ex defectu juris in agente". How logically conclusive is an argument prohibiting an act because it is performed "ex defectu juris in agente"?

AN APPRAISAL OF THE ARGUMENT WHICH STATES THAT AN ACT IS MORALLY WRONG BECAUSE IT IS PERFORMED - EX DEFECTU JURIS IN AGENTE

Like many manualists, F. Regatillo and M. Zalba (48) argue against suicide in the following manner:

"destructio alicuius rei est actus dominii, et suicida cui sola competit utilitas, sibi arrogat ipsam substantiam vitae, eam subtrahens domino divino."

Some moralists (49) are of the opinion that this argument is logically inconclusive. First, a pure semantic analysis of the statement reveals that "to have dominion over a thing" is synonymous with the right of destroying it or the right of disposing of it. Thus the statement: "Man has no right to take away his life because he has no right of dominion over himself" is semantically equivalent to: "Man has no right to take away his life because he has no right to destroy himself." The tautological nature of this statement reveals the fallacy, petitio principii, on which the argument is founded. Far from offering

---

47 Mausbach and Ermecke, ibid., 253, argue: "Der Mensch kann nämlich kein Eigentum an seinem Leben haben:
1. weil Eigentum die Herrschaftsbefugnis über Sachgüter ist. Der Leib des lebendigen Menschen ist keine Sache, sondern eins mit seiner Person ...
2. weil das, worauf sich Eigentum erstreckt, etwas vom Eigentümer seinsmäßig verschiedenes, getrenntes sein muß. Der Leib ist aber Mensch selbst in der Existenz seines Leibes."
48 F. Regatillo and M. Zalba, op. cit., vol. 2, nr. 248, p. 258.
49 see B. Schüller, Die Begründung, pp. 236 ff; R. Ginters, Werte und Normen, pp. 58-60.

a reason why a man ought not to kill himself, the argument simply states: While God may kill a man, a man may not kill himself or stated in other words: an act which a man may not perform, God may perform it.

Second, the argument presents the rights of God as Creator and the rights of man as creature not in an analogical but in an univocal manner. The rights a man exercises over his "creation" or material possession excludes others from having the same right. A man's right, seen in this way, stands in contest with the rights of others. Thus to have a right over some material good means the same as saying that no other person possesses this right. It is evident that here the right which God, as Creator, has over man, his creature, is thought to be similar to that which a man exercises over his "creation". If Michaelangelo has the right to dispose of his Pieta, since it is his creation, no other one is in possession of such a right. If God has the right to dispose of life, since life is his creation, then man cannot simultaneously possess this right. It is obvious from the doctrine of creation that God as "Causa Prima" cannot be rightly thought of as a cause among other causes (causae secundae). The relationship between a Creator and his creation is unique. God's rights can not be seen as contesting with the rights of men.

Third, if the argument which states that a man should not kill himself or any other innocent person because only God who possesses right of dominion over human life has right to dispose of it, were to be seen as conclusive, it should also apply to all destructions of human life whether innocent or not because God, as creator of all, exercises such dominion and right over all. In fact, the argument should apply to the disposal of all creatures. Arguing in a parallel manner one will say that since God, as Creator exercises the right of ownership over all acres of land on earth no one may dispose of a parcel of land. Doing so is usurping God's sovereign rights. This seems absurd.

Lastly, the right of ownership applies only to material things. Man, as a person with the power and right of self-determination, cannot be owned or disposed of as a material possession.

From the foregoing it is evident that asserting that an act is morally wrong because it is performed "ex defectu juris in agente" or because only God has a right to perform such an act can be said to be logically inconclusive. The killing of an innocent person as well as mutilation could be seen as morally wrong for reasons other than saying they are performed "ex defectu juris in agente".

Since Catholic tradition teaches that a proportionate grave reason can justify mutilation as well as the disposal of human life in self-defence, in war, in executing a capital punishment, in letting an innocent person die and in killing an innocent man with an indirect intention, it follows logically that it neither considers mutilation nor the destruction of human life as the causation of an absolute (moral) evil. It sees each of them as the causing of non-moral evils. Direct mutilation and direct killing of an innocent person are names designating acts of mutilation and killing respectively which tradition believes are performed without a proportionate reason. In contrast, indirect mutilation and indirect killing describe acts justifiable for a proportionate reason. In using a proportionate reason to norm such acts, Catholic tradition conceeds that consequences play a moral significant role in determining their moral quality.

3.3. THE DIRECT/INDIRECT DISTINCTION: A RESTRICTIVE INTERPRETATION OF DEONTOLOGICAL NORMS

Since killing is permitted in war, in self-defence and in the execution of capital punishment, one may take the deontological prohibition of killing to refer to the destruction of the life of an innocent person and so state this norm as follows: "Thou shall not kill an innocent person". Since the word "innocent" can refer to oneself or to another, the deontological prohibition of killing could be stated as follows: "You should neither kill yourself nor another innocent person". Furthermore, since it is generally believed that one is accountable for deaths resulting from one's personal decision, "killing" may be understood as "taking a decision whose execution is foreseen as resulting in one's death or in another's". If this provisional definition of killing is acceded to, then the deontological prohibition of killing could be stated as follows: "You ought not to take a decision whose execution is foreseen to result in your own death or in that of some innocent person". Applied to practical life this definition evidently leads to contradictory and unacceptable consequences.

A few concrete examples may help illuminate this point. A, finds life an intolerable burden and so decides to swallow an overdose of sleeping tablets that made him "sleep in peace" and thereby put an end to his burden. B, in order to avoid a rather cruel death by fire, decides to jump through a window of the sixth floor of a burning building, foreseeing that this would necessarily result in his death. C, a priest in a concentration camp, takes the place of a father of a family condemned to death, although he foresees that his death will necessarily follow from this decision. These are decisions whose execution are foreseen to result in one's death. Tradition considers A's act immoral. Conversely, it deems B's deed morally permissible and C's heroic and praiseworthy. Thus B's and C's cases stand as counter examples to the overriding validity of the above deontological prohibition of killing.

Two concrete examples of acts that result in the death of another would suffice to add further light to this point. D, a doctor, decides to perform an ectopic operation, foreseeing that the death of the fetus will necessarily follow. E, another doctor, decides to omit a similar operation, foreseeing that the death of the fetus will follow. Were the deontological prohibition of killing of the innocent described above to be applied to these cases, D's and E's actions will be condemned as morally objectionable. Thus actions which relate to one another as contradictories will both be judged morally wrong at the same time and in similar situations. But the truth-values of contradictory propositions are such that, if one is false, the other will necessarily be true. Both can neither be simultaneously true nor simultaneously false. In the same vein, D's and E's actions which relate to each other as contradictories cannot be both morally wrong at the same time and under similar circumstances; if one is morally wrong, the other will necessarily be morally right. From this, it is apparent that contradictory and unacceptable conclusions will follow were the above deontological prohibition to apply strictly to all these cases.

Moralists of the catholic tradition were aware of such contradictions and the extreme hardships which a strict interpretation of deontological prohibitions will give rise to. Consequently, they took steps to obviate these adversities by narrowing down the scope or range of deontological proscriptions in such a manner that a prohibition like "thou shall not kill an innocent person inspite of the consequences" becomes inoffensive even to one opposed to the deontoligical method of grounding ethical norms. Some modern theologians like Schüller (50) call this benign way of understanding a deontological prohibition in order to avoid its unpalatable consequences, "a restrictive interpretation of a deontological norm".

The principle of double effect with its direct/indirect distinction serves catholic moralists the purpose of a restrictive interpretation of deontological norms. Before demonstrating this fact, with reference to the deontological prohibition of killing, it will be rewarding to illustrate how a "restrictive interpretation" functions in practice by examining the treatment of lying (mendacium) by catholic moralists.

3.3.1. LYING (MENDACIUM) AS A PARADIGMATIC ILLUSTRATION OF A RESTRICTIVE INTERPRETATION OF A MORAL NORM

No one contends that each person has a duty to be truthful. Similarly, nobody disputes that a man has the right to preserve his secrets or even the duty to conceal the secrets of others. In some instances keeping a secret is a test of truthfulness and fidelity, since some secrets are entrusted to some people under the implicit or explicit promise that they will not be violated. In other instances, particularly in cases relating to natural secrets, prudence, justice or charity forbids one to reveal the facts of a case to a third party. While one has the duty to conceal certain secrets, one has simultaneously the obligation of being truthful. What happens when one cannot tell the truth without betraying an important secret that can, for instance, cost a human life or when one cannot keep a secret and still speak truthfully?

In replying to this question moralists propound diverse opinions. In such a situation some will permit the telling of an officious lie and the use of a pure mental reservation. Catholic moralists are of the view that while the use of a broad mental reservation and silence are morally permissible, the telling of falsehood (mendacium) whatever

---

50 cf. B. Schüller, **Die Begründung**, pp. 177 ff.

the consequences is morally proscribed. Equally they deem the use of a pure mental restriction morally prohibited since they consider it a form of lying (mendacium). From this it seems that in the Catholic tradition, the making of a false statement (mendacium) is viewed as prohibited without exception.

This prohibition of falsehood may be stated as follows: "You may never make a false statement (mendacium) whatever the consequences". The practical importance of this proposition as a normative guide hangs on what one understands by the word "mendacium". The definition of this term by catholic moralists of the past is traceable to the writings of Saints Augustine of Hippo and Thomas Aquinas.

Augustine deals with the problem of lying extensively in two of his works: **De Mendacio** (395) and **Contra Mendacium** (420). In the latter he maintains that "mendacium est quippe falsa significatio cum voluntate fallendi" (51). The Scholastics adopted this definition. Many in this school of thought did not consider "the intention to deceive" a "differentia specifica" of lying. St. Thomas, for instance, takes "mendacium" simply to mean "locutio contra mentem" and says that the intention to deceive "non pertinet ad speciem mendacii sed ad quandam perfectionem ipsius" (52). He stresses that the essence of lying (mendacium) consists in the intention to tell what one believes to be false. Thus in his view, a statement which is opposed to the truth as known by the speaker is a lie, whether the speaker intends to deceive anyone or not. Also a lie is told if one deliberately makes a true statement which he mistakenly believes to be false (53).

Although the essential determinant of a lie is the intention to speak falsely, nevertheless, the intention to deceive is objectively present in each lie "ex parte operis". One who performs an act which produces a particular effect from its very nature intends this effect

---

51 Augustine, Contra Mendacium XII, 26, P.L., 40, 537.

52 Thomas Aquinas, S. Th., II–II, q. 110, a. 1. Most manuals of moral theology adopt Thomas' view and maintain that 'the intention to deceive' does not belong to the essence of 'mendacium'. Cf. Otto Schilling, **Grundriss der Moraltheologie**, Freiburg, Herder 2 ed. 1949, nr. 371, and Mausbach-Ermecke, op. cit., vol. iii, pp. 593-594.

53 Nicholai Hartmann, **Ethik**, Berlin 1962, p. 460 stresses the same point when he says: "Und der Lügner kann sehr wohl die Wahrheit sagen, nämlich wider Willen, indem er Wahres für unwahr hält. Denn der Sinn der Lüge ist nicht für wahr auszugeben, was unwahr ist, sondern was man für unwahr hält. So kommt es, daß wahre Rede doch Lüge sein kann."

at least in its cause (54).

Remaining faithful to the definition of lying by Augustine and Thomas one may formulate the deontological prohibition of "mendacium" as follows: "You should never deliberately make a statement you believe to be false whether or not you intend to deceive the listener". Since Catholic tradition deems the use of a veiled speech or broad mental reservation a legitimate means of treading through the "Sylla and Charybdis" which exists when the duty of "never-make-a-false-statement" conflicts with that of keeping a secret, it means that a veiled speech is not to be understood as "mendacium". Therefore it is to be excluded from the ambient of what tradition understands as "mendacium". The implication of this exclusion will become clearer when the nature of a broad mental reservation is analysed.

Contrasting a broad mental reservation with a pure mental reservation brings the nature of the former into deep relief. A pure mental restriction consists in stating something untrue in words and merely adding a correction or qualification of the same in the mind or very softly that the speaker only knows of it. An example. Someone is asked: "Have you seen Rome?". He replies, "Yes", adding in his mind "on a picture". Catholic tradition considers a pure mental restriction a species of "mendacium" and so it was formally condemned by Innocent XI in 1679 (55).

On the other hand, a broad mental restriction consists in making a statement which has two senses: one true, the other false (56). A famous illustration of this is that given by Felix of Nola (57). When asked by his persecutors – who failed to recognize him – whether he knew Felix, he answered "Nescio Felicem quem quaeritis". This reply has at least two meanings:

1) I do not know Felix whom you are seeking;

2) I do not know the happy man you are seeking, implying that, I know that the man you are seeking is unhappy.

----

54 See also A. Kern, **Die Lüge**, Graz 1930, p. 7.

55 cf. D. 1176–1178.

56 Regarding the broad mental restriction Noldin and Smith say: "Alii meliorem modum proposuerunt, adhibendi scil. Verba, quae duplicem sensum admittunt, ita ut sint uno sensu vera, altero falsa. Et cum loquens primum sensum in mente habeat, non mentitur, sed ponit actionem in se licitam, quae habet duplicem effectum, quorum unus, occultatio veritatis, intenditur, alter, deceptio interrogantis, praeter intentionem est. Talem modum loquendi postea vocabant **restrictionem late mentalem**, ..." Smith-Noldin, op. cit., vol. 2, pp. 589–590.

57 Cf. Karl Hörmann, **An Introduction to Moral Theology**, London 1961, p. 269.

Seen in isolation, the first is a "locutio contra mentem" since Felix knows Felix (himself). The second statement is a "locutio secundum mentem", because Felix knows that he is unhappy (not "felix") in the face of his persecutors. In order that the mental reservation be legitimate, Felix has to intend the second meaning of the statement while permitting (prayerfully though) that the inquirer understand the first.

This analysis reveals that the broad mental reservation has an ambiguous character. Considered from it's second meaning there is an "adaequatio rei et intellectus", thus, it is a permitted act. Judged from its first meaning, it is a statement known by Felix to be false. This meaning of the statement coincides with a lie (mendacium). Thus a broad mental reservation seems to be at once a true and a false statement.

Since such statements are excluded from the range of "mendacium", the definition of the latter needs some qualification or rather needs to be narrowed down. Thus it could be further reconstructed as follows: "You should never make a statement you believe to be false whether or not you intend to deceive the listener unless the statement is ambiguous in character".

It is a known fact that the theory of mental restriction has its limitation and drawbacks. To use this means demands a lot of wit as well as a presence of mind that is often out of the reach of the average man. One who has only a little command of a particular language may not quickly find an appropriate "restriction" and could be much handicapped in its use. Moreover, an attentive and intelligent listener may not be led into error by it. He may discover the ambiguity in the reply and press for more clarification and precision. Above and beyond, the theory of mental restriction is seen to be of no practical use in a situation where an inquirer leaves a person only with the alternatives of either a "Yes" or a "No". A modified example from E. Welty (58) may help to bring such a situation in clear light.

A military personal lays violent hands on an unblemished girl. Her father promptly intervenes. After a violent fight he succeeds in pushing the officer down the steps. The latter falls, breaks his neck and dies. Father and daughter know clearly well that they would end up in the gallows should they describe exactly the running of events. What should they do in such a case? In reply to this question it is necessary to keep in mind that in a totalitarian State Court procedures are scrupulously manipulated, and what is more, the State habitually uses the facts it gets to persecute innocent persons. Furthermore, it is necessary to recall that if a person avoids giving an answer or if he makes evasive statements he is quickly condemned as a defaulter and promptly executed. Only a "Yes" or a "No" can either save or claim the necks of those concerned.

It will be stressing the obvious to say that the theory of broad mental restriction is unable to cope up with a situation like this.

----

58 cf. G. Müller, **Die Wahrhaftigkeitspflicht und die Lüge**, Freiburg 1962, p. 4.

Faced with similar situations some catholic moralists of the past and present times seek a way out of this moral quandary by approving of the making of a false statement (particularly telling of officious lie) in emergency situations.

One effect of this tendency of permitting the making of false statements in emergency is that these theologians are compelled to narrow down the scope of the traditional understanding of "mendacium" in order to hold to its absolute prohibition. Some of these theologians would understand "mendacium" to entail the intention to deceive a person who has a right to be truth (59). For a proportionate reason they maintain, one may make a false statement to an indiscreet questioner who has no right to knowing the facts of a case (60).

In order to narrow down the traditional definition of "mendacium", Lindworsky (61) finds it necessary to refute first and foremost the traditional argument which asserts that the intrinsic evil nature of lying consists in its vitiation of the function of speech (communication of one's mind to another). He argues that speech is not a ready-made gift from nature, nor something that originated through the agreement of men but a discovery of man. Therefore, neither through its essence nor through its foundation can one determine which function is contrary to its nature. He points out that the functions of speech are many. It can serve as a means of expression, as a means of influencing others, as a means of manifesting our conviction, as a means of self-defence – as for example, through threatening the other – and also as a means of leading others into error. If it is necessary to talk of one function of speech one can describe it as a "Hilfsmittel für das Leben".

----

59 G. Müller, op. cit., p. 327, points out that theologians who propound the theory of "the right to the truth" include eminent moralists like Tanquery, Kelly, Ruland an so on. They have Hugo Grotius and Pufendorf as their forerunners who distinguished between "falsiloquum" and "mendacium". "Falsiloquum" consists simply in the making of a false statement. "Mendacium" consists in making a statement believed to be false to one with a right to the truth. Cf. A. Kern, op. cit., pp. 8-13. Schüller, **Die Begründung**, p. 178, rightly points out that moralists that propound the theory of "the right to the truth" simply make analytic statements. If a person has no right to the truth, a speaker has no obligation of telling him the truth.

60 A. Vermeersch, "De mendacio et necessitatibus commercii humani". Gregorianum, 1 (1920), 11-40, 425-475, for instance, justifies the use of falsehood in an emergency situation by drawing a parallel between the killing of an unjust aggressor in self-defence and the telling of falsehood to an indiscreet questioner. Just as one is permitted to kill in self-defence, one is allowed to make a false statement to an indiscreet questioner in an emergency situation.

61 J. Lindworsky, "Das Problem der Lüge bei katholischen Ethikern und Moralisten". Otto Lipmann and Paul Plaut (ed), **Die Lüge**, Leipzig 1927, p. 56 ff.

It would be mistaking a part for its whole to say that the nature or function of Speech consists in manifesting one's mind to the other. A fortiori it would also be fallacious to argue that one who makes a false statement has vitiated the nature of speech or has acted contrary to nature. Disagreeing with the traditional argument on which the prohibition of false statements is grounded and also the traditional definition of "mendacium", Lindworsky offers a different definition when he says:

> "Von einer Lüge wird man somit reden, wenn zur Darstellung eines Sachverhalts bewußt und gewollt die Kundgabe einer nicht vorhandenen Überzeugung von der Existenz des Sachverhalts tritt." (62)

The foregoing pages reveal that catholic moralists of the past are not strangers to the hard facts of life. They are cognizant of the problems posed in daily life by a prohibition of false statements which admits no exceptions. To mitigate or even remove the problems completely they take steps to widen the scope where acts of falsehood are permitted for a proportionate reason. Correspondingly they narrow down the area where the prohibition of the making of a false statement is binding without exception. Accordingly by making the prohibition of false statement practically harmless, they are able to cope up wit the problems of daily life that challenge the obligation of never-make-a-false-statement.

3.3.2. THE DIRECT/INDIRECT DISTINCTION EMPLOYED AS A RESTRICTIVE INTERPRETATION OF DEONTOLOGICAL PROHIBITION OF KILLING

Human life is said to be sacred and inviolable. What is meant by this is not that human life cannot be destroyed but rather that it ought not be destroyed. Why should human life not be destroyed? The usual reply catholic tradition gives to this question, as has already been seen, is that man, by destroying human life, acts beyond his power and so violates the inalienable right of God, who, as Lord over life and death, has the prerogative of specifying the time of death for each man. Following this traditional argument strictly leads to the the conclusion that God's sovereign right is usurped whenever human life is destroyed. It is no less so if the life in question is that of an unjust aggressor or a blood-thirsty tyrant or a duly condemned criminal or the lives of soldiers carrying out an unjust war.

Catholic tradition is cognizant of what enormous threat an absolute prohibition of killing in every instance will pose to the general welfare of humanity, so it distinguishes first, between killing innocent and non-innocent persons. By "non-innocent" catholic tradition

----

62 ibid., pp. 69-70.

understands people like unjust aggressors, duly condemned criminals who are guilty of grave crimes and soldiers engaged in an unjust war. It believes that God sometimes delegates His sovereign rights to men or to human authorities in instances pertaining to the killing of such non-innocent persons.

One may kill an unjust aggressor if that is the only effective way open to one to protect oneself, one's vital goods spritual and temporal, or the lives of one's dependants. One may kill soldiers in war if that is the only means to warding off their unjust aggression. A competent authority also may kill a duly condemned criminal guilty of a grave crime if that is the only way of protecting society against his threats.

In these instances the destruction of human life is not arbitrary; it is done for a proportionate reason. Man, as it were, using God's precious gift of reason, weighs the various alternatives open to him and discovers that God wants him to protect an important value by sacrificing a lesser or an equally important value, namely, a human life. Thus when the destruction of non-innocent person is in question, catholic tradition interpretes the prohibition of killing a human being teleologically.

With the exclusion of the killing of non-innocent persons from the ambient of the deontological norm prohibiting killing, it might look like this norm binds without exception in cases involving innocent human life. If this were to be the case, innocent human life will be deemed the greatest value and the norm prohibiting its destruction would demand that one is not to do or omit anything from which the death of an innocent person is foreseen to follow. What consequences will follow from this?

A man for instance, would have the moral obligation of sacrificing all the resources of his family in order to save the life of a terminally sick relative, even if continued existence is an excruciating anguish for the sick. What grim or contradictory consequences such state of affairs has in stock are obvious. For instance, by sacrificing all the resources of his family to prolong the life of an incurable sick relative, a man puts his life and the lives of other members of his family in jeopardy. Thus in trying to save one human life more lives are lost.

To obviate such undesirable consequences catholic tradition distinguishes again between "killing" and "letting-die". It believes that God further delegates some of his sovereign rights to man and empowers him to omit certain actions that would have otherwise saved innocent human life. Thus it teaches that it is lawful for a doctor to omit carrying out an expensive operation that would bring the relatives of a patient into bankruptcy (passive euthanasia). By judging "letting-die" according to teleological methodology, catholic tradition takes a further step in restricting the ambient of the prohibition of killing that is to be understood as a deontological norm.

Having excluded killing of non-innocent persons and letting-die form the range of the proscription of killing understood as a deontological norm, it would seem that this norm will aways be binding where positive acts of killing innocent persons are concerned.

But this is not the case. Within the realm of positive acts of kill-ing Tradition makes a subtle distinction between direct and indirect killing. It assesses indirect killing teleologically. By making this move it limits the deontological appraisal to direct killing. The re-stricted area where the deontological norm applies is projected in the following figure:

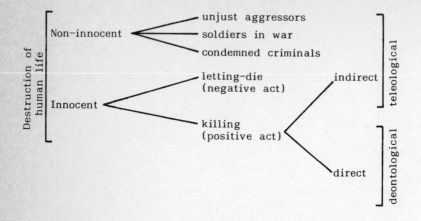

The way and manner Tradition attempts to interpret the deontolo-gical norms restrictively by means of the direct/indirect distinction may be conretely illustrated with reference to two controversies.

1) The controversy over direct and indirect abortion;

2) The controversy over direct and indirect willing of "per se" effects.

3.3.2.1. The controversy over direct and indirect abortion between 16th – 18th centuries

3.3.2.1.1. Vasquez

Germain G. Grisez (63) and John Connery (64) observe that one of the difficult problems that engaged the minds of moralists between the sixteenth and eighteenth centuries was the problem of abortion to save the mother. Gabriel Vasquez (65) (1569-1649) in his contribution to the discussion of the problem defends a rather strict opinion. He is of the view that all abortions, whether of animated or non-animated foetus, whether direct or indirect resulting from a positive act are morally objectionable. He insists that one may not do any thing in a direct line of cause – effect relation that leads to the death of the foetus. In instances of an abortion to save the mother, one is only permitted to treat the mother in ways that incidentally and only negatively affect the life of the foetus, as for example, by inhibiting its nutrition.

It is evident that were Vasquez to formulate the deontological prohibition of killing he would present it exactly as it was provisionally stated above, that is to say, "You should never perform a positive act foreseen to result in the death of an innocent person."

3.3.2.1.2. Juan de Lugo

In 1642 Juan de Lugo (66) adopts the view of Vasquez and modifies it to a certain degree. He follows the stricter view of Vasquez in cases where the foetus is animated. He, however, qualifies this with restrictions aimed at the spiritual good of the child, if delay can make its live-birth and baptism possible. In cases where the foetus is not animated he parts company with Vasquez and adopts a more moderate view. In such instances he employs the principle of indirect intention and permits treatments necessary to cure the woman even though they may have abortificient side effects.

----

63 Germain G. Grisez, **Abortion: The Myths, the Realities and the Arguments**, New York Corpus Books 1970, pp. 165 ff.

64 John Connery, **Abortion: The Development of the Roman Catholic Perspective**, Loyola, Uni. press 1977, pp. 130 ff. See also John Dedek, **Human Life, Some Moral Issues**, New York Sheed and Ward 1972, p. 40.

65 Gabriel Vasquez, **Opuscula moralia**, "De Restitutione", cap. 3, p. 2, dub. 6.

66 Juan de Lugo S.J., **Disputationes scholasticae et morales vol VI, De iustitiae et iure**, (Paris 1869), disp. 10, sect. 5.

Thus, in the eyes of Juan de Lugo the above provisional definition of the deontological prohibition of killing is valid only in so far as it applies to a foetus that is animated. Where the foetus is not animated, it is not. Juan de Lugo subjects an act of killing of this type to teleological appraisal. By doing this, he narrows down the scope of the deontological prohibition of killing as understood by Gabriel Vasquez.

3.3.2.1.3. The Salmanticenses

Reviewing theological literatures of the past, the Salmanticenses (67) maintain that hardly anything can be defined as certain about the time of animation and teach that at every stage of pregnancy, a woman may use means directly ordered to restore her health even if abortion is likely to result. The Salmanticenses argue that the death of the child in the case is indirectly willed and may thus be permitted for a proportionate reason. By arguing that the principle of indirect voluntary extends to all stages of pregnancy regardless of the animation of the foetus and also that an indirectly willed abortion may be permitted for a proportionate reason, they silently rejected the stricter opinions of Vasquez and Juan de Lugo.

Thus, the Salmanticenses would narrow down the extention of the above definition of deontological proscription of killing by making a subtle distinction between direct and indirect killing of an innocent person. Indirect killing of an innocent person is removed from this area and subjected to teleological appraisal.

3.3.2.2. The controversy over direct and indirect willing of "per se" effects between 16th – 17th centuries

One of the results yielded by the analysis of the nature of acts governed by the principle of double effects is that acts which produce "per se" effects are appraised deontologically, while those with "per accidens" effects are assessed teleologically. In the 16th and 17th centuries, there was an interesting and rigorous debate among theologians on whether the natural (per se) and accidental effects could be the object of indirect voluntariness.

The context of this debate was Thomas' treatment of killing in self-defence in **Summa Theologica** II-II, q 64,a.7. Here Thomas distinguishes between intentional and unintentional killing in self-defence.

----

67 Collegii Salmanticensis, **Cursus theologiae moralis**, III (Venice 1728), tr. 13, cap. 2, punct. 4.

The former is always morally wrong, the latter is morally wrong if due moderation is not observed. If unintended killing is unlawful under certain conditions, evidently it is considered a voluntary act, for only that which is voluntary can be classed as morally lawful or unlawful (68). Here are two acts of the will dealing with the same object. If the object is intended the act is considered morally wrong. If the object flows from the will "praeter intentionem" (indirectly) it is not always morally wrong. Evidently, this difference in the moral character of the act is due to the manner in which the will acts upon the object. The question that engaged the minds of theologians then was: What types of objects (per se or per accidens effects) can form the object of indirect voluntary.

Regarding the possibility of an effect "per accidens" (69) constituting the object of indirect voluntary, theologians commonly shared the same view. Suarez (70), for instance, argues that accidental effects are not inseparably connected with their causes because the effects depend on the concurrence of other causes, which in the hypothesis are not willed. Therefore, that which is willed does not virtually contain the effect. To be voluntary, an accidental effect has to be more closely connected with its cause. This connection is not physical but moral and is attained by a command or precept forbidding the cause on account of the effect. Put in a different way, unintended accidental effects are not voluntary, unless their cause is expressly forbidden on account of the effects.

Similarly the Salmanticenses argue that only effects (per se or per accidens) which the will can and must avoid are to be considered indirectly willed and attributed to the will (71). However, for a proportionate reason, it is lawful to actuate a cause which produces such unlawful effects if they are merely foreseen but not intended. The agent permitting the illegal effect is considered "morally impotent" to impede it and is consequently, excused from moral obligation (72).

----

68 Thomas Aquinas, Summa contr. Gent., lib. 3, c. 9: "Secundum hoc enim aliquid ad genus moris pertinet, quod est voluntarium".

69 Although acts that produce effects "per accidens", that is to say, acts appraised teleologically are not our main concern here, I consider referring to them briefly here appropriate for two reasons. First, this survey reveals that theologians of the past had no difficulty or disagreement in applying the principle of indirect voluntary to them. Second, theologians of the past considered the principle of indirect voluntary applicable not to all acts but only to acts that produce illegal or intrinsic evil effects.

70 Suarez, De volunatrium et involunatrium, 1, sec. 4, nn. 8-9, in: **Opera Omnia** vol. IV, ed. Carolus Berton, Parisiis 1856, "Secundo addendum est, quando effectus sequitur tantum posteriori modo, ut censeatur volunatris in alio, necessariam esse obligationem vitandi unum ne sequatur aliud, ... et ratio est, quia ut aliquid sit volunatrium, prout nunc de illo agimus, necessarium in primis est, ut sit volitum, ed deinde ut sit aliquo modo a voluntate: nihil autem hic invenitur seculo praecepto."

71 Salmanticenses, op. cit., tr. 13, disp. 10, n. 241.

72 ibid., n. 244.

The term "evil effect", "unlawful effect" and "illegal effect" which appear repeatedly in the treatment of the voluntary nature of "per accidens" effects, as well as "per se" effects, present some ambiguities which could be misleading. A closer examination of the texts reveals that the terms are used as synonyms. Generally to say that an effect is illegal or unlawful is another way of stating that the production of such is prohibited. Some of the questions that immediately come to mind here are:

a) Is the effect evil because it is prohibited? or

b) Is the effect evil in itself and so prohibited? or

c) Is the act of producing such an effect evil and so prohibited? Putting it in a different way,

Is producing such an effect intrinsically evil?

An examination of the examples of evil mentioned in the text, namely scandal, taking of veneral pleasure, pollution, homicide, leads to the conclusion that the evils in question are those considered intrinsic (moral) evils by tradition. Hence it is demanded that these evil or illegal effects may never be intended, even in cases where a proportionate reason allows their causation.

Regarding the possibility of an effect "per se" constituting the object of indirect voluntary, theological opinions are divided. Some theologians like Suarez defend the view that an effect "per se" cannot be indirectly willed. Others, like the School of Salmanticenses, argue that in some cases they could be permitted for a grave reason. What arguments do they employ to support their views?

3.3.2.2.1. Franciscus Suarez

In the opinion of Francis Suarez an effect "per se" is so intimately connected with its cause that both are considered but a single object of the will such that he who wills the cause necessarily wills the effect virtually contained in it. Thus every effect "per se" can only be directly willed and consequently cannot be the object of indirect voluntary. He continues by making a statement which is analytically true:

> "Si effectus verbi gratia, prohibitus sit, necesse est, ut sit etiam prohibita causa, ex qua per se, et ex praecisa virtute illius sequitur talis effectus". (73)

Thus if the production of an effect is forbidden as immoral intending its cause should also be considered immoral.

----

73 Suarez, op. cit., 1, sec. 4, nn. 8-9.

Traces of the teaching of Suarez are discernable in Dominicus Prümmer's (74) formulation of the principle of double effect. In contradistinction to authors who state one of the conditions of the principle as: The good effect should at least proceed from the act as immediately as the evil effect, Prümmer asserts:

"2. Deinde requiritur, ut bonus effectus sit immediatus, i.e. ut malus effectus non praecedat, sed sequitur illum. Patet ex textu S. Pauli 'Non facimus mala, ut veniat bona'".

From this, Prümmer draws the conclusion that if the natural (per se) effect of an act is evil, everything proceeding from this act would be evil, since it would follow by means of this "per se" evil effect. The possibility is lacking, he continues, that an evil and a good effect flow with equal immediacy from an act, since every act is of a single species and, by its nature, produce only a single effect. If the effect is evil, no good can ever justify the use of the evil means. If this effect is good, and the end it serves good, any evil effect that follows later because of the interference of some other cause is only accidental to the will.

Prümmer's argument as well as that of Suarez, which states that an act can only have one natural effect is drawn from Thomas Aquinas's **Summa Theologica** 1-2, q. 1, a. 3, ad. 3. Here Thomas teaches that the end specifies an act and asserts that the natural end of an act gives it its principal determination or species.

The second argument of Suarez is drawn from the familiar axiom which states that he who intends the cause intends also the effect or as it is often formulated: "Causa causae est causa causati".

The two arguments presented by Suarez call for some closer examination. But first it is worthwhile to stress that the union between a "causa per se" and its natural effects stressed by Suarez, although inseparable "in re" is separable intellectually. For the intellect is capable of distinguishing between a cause and its effect even when they are very intimately connected. It is not true that he who wills a cause also necessarily wills the effects essentially connected with it. A cause could be willed as a "causa quae causa", that is to say, only in so far as it is a cause. In contrast, a cause could be willed as a "causa qua causa" that is to say in so far as it is the cause of an effect such that when it is willed its effect is also willed.

Second, Suarez's assertion that an evil and a good effect can not simultaneously flow "per se" from an act does not agree with the evidence of common experience. The "per se" effects of some acts must be considered either as being many or as distinct from one another. A bomb explosion on a fortress causes the death of innocent civilians as immediately as the death of combatants (which immediately entails the ceasation of hostilities) and each independent of the other.

---

74 Dominicus Prümmer, **Manuale Theologiae Moralis**, p. 46.

The first argument of Suarez as has been indicated is based on Summa Theologica 1-2, q. 1, a. 3, ad. 3. Attempts at explaining what Thomas intends by this text has led to controversies. In the main two solutions have been offered.

The first holds that Thomas is here distinguishing between the method in which the species of natural acts and the species of moral acts is determined. Any act of a natural agent is determined to one specific end, he says, by the very nature of that agent, and therefore a given act may be said to receive its species either from what the agent "intends" or from what the agent actually effects, for the two will always be the same. But the will, the principle of human causality, is not determined to any single object, but can determine itself to any object. Therefore the human act receives its species not from what the agent does, but from that to which he determines himself, that which he chooses. For this reason, St. Thomas adds that an act when considered as a natural act may be of another species (75).

The second solution holds that by the "finis" which determines the "speciem naturae" Thomas has in mind the end as the essential and intrinsic nature of the act. The end which gives the act its natural species is so intimately a part of the act that it must be chosen by the will. All acts are said to be specified by their proximate ends. If the act is chosen, it must be chosen because of what it does, because of this proximate natural end. That effect which always

----

75 "Principia activa esse varia. Quaedam sunt naturaliter determinata ad eosdem actus; sicut sol ad illuminandum, calor ad califaciendum, frigus ad infrigidandum, alia non sunt naturaliter determinata, sicut ratio et voluntas. Quod autem B. Thomas ait, actiones specificari a principio activo; verum est de principio prioris generis. Cum enim ejusmodi principium sit determinatum ad producendum effectum sibi consimilem: effectus autem ille sit terminus actionis; manifestum est illam actionem specificari non solum ex termino sed etiam ex principio activo, quia principium est ejusdem rationis cum termino. Sed in principio posterioris generis aliter res se habet, quia tale principium non est ex necessitate determinatum ad unum; et propterea potest causare actus diversae speciei, sicut eadem potentia voluntatis nunc bonus nunc malo, eosque, diversissimos actus producit: imo et eadem prava voluntas etiam ex eodem timore male humilante potest causare furtum, homicidium, gregis commissi desertionem, et alia hujusmodi. Unde manifestum est, quod actiones voluntariae non differant specie, secundum diversas causas activas; ideoque non sortiantur speciem ex principio effectivo, sed solum secundum diversitatem causae finalis." Sylvius, Comm. in Summam Theol., I-II, q. 1, a. 3; See also Dumas, Theol. Moral Thomistica, vol. 1, (Paris 1930), p. 15; Ludovicus Billot, De Personalis et Originali Peccato, (Rome 1924), pp. 52-53.

and necessarily follows from an act, gives it its species and must be chosen along with the act even though the act is also directed to some ulterior ends (76).

When discussing the effects of acts, St. Thomas again says that the natural evil effects of acts increases the evil of the act, even if the effect is not foreseen or intended. The same statement is also made regarding good acts with good consequences (77). It is to be noted in the first place, that St. Thomas in both cases, is speaking of agumenting the moral quality that the act already possesses, and not giving it its first moral character or changing what it already has. In the second place, to say that an act receives its moral determination from an effect is not equivalent to saying that the effect must be directly willed. It may be willed only indirectly. Moreover, Thomas asserts that these effects increase the moral species even if they are nor foreseen. Yet no one will admit that we can have a human act without intellectual knowledge of the object of the act.

A better explanation seems to be that Thomas had in mind effects that are a sign rather than the cause of the moral character of the act in question so that the cause has more good or evil effects because of its own intrinsic goodness or badness (78). Thomas states that an act is better "ex genere suo" from which many good effects follow, and another is worse from which more evil can follow. Or again, in **Summa Theologica** 1-2, q. 73, a. 8 he states that the gravity of the evil effects does not make the sin more grave, but it is because the sin in itself is so serious that it has so many evil effects.

----

76 "Auctor non negat pluralitatem finum etiam proximorum absolute, sed specificantium actum. Unius enim numero actus, prout semel egreditur ab operante (quod dicitur propter accidentes intentiones in continando actum), unus solus est finis proprius, a quo est species velut substantialis." Thomas de Vio Cajetan, Comm. in I-II, q. 1, a. 3, ad. 3, in: **Commentaria in Summa Theologicam S. Thomae Aquinatis**, (Romae 1882). Medina in his **Expositio in Primam Secundam Angelici Doctoris**, Venice 1590), I-II, q. 1, a. 3, mentions both opinions and prefers the second.

77 "Si autem eventus sequens non sit praecogitatus, tunc distinguendum est. Quia si per se sequitur ex tali actu, et ut in pluribus, secundum hoc eventus sequens addit ad bonitatem vel malitiam actus: Manifestum est enim meliorem actum esse ex suo genere, ex quo possunt plura bona sequi; et pejorem ex quo nata sunt plura mala sequi." S. Th., I-II, q. 20, a. 5. See also S. Th., I-II, q. 73, a. 8.

78 cf. Medina, op. cit., I-II, q. 73, a. 1; Salmanticensis, op. cit., tr. 13, disp. 10, dub. 4, n. 162.

The second argument of Suarez is based on the axiom: "Causa causae est causa causati". This axiom is true when the causes in question are of the same species, as for instance, a series of efficient causes or a series of final causes; but not if it is applied to a mixed series of efficient and final causes (79). Accelerating a car is the cause of the revolution of its wheels, which in turn is the cause of the wear and tear of the tyres. The acceleration caused by the driver is properly seen as the efficient cause of this wear and tear . The driver fuels the car in order that it would be able to accelerate. While it will be right to view the acceleration of the car as the final cause of fueling it, it would be wrong to assert that the driver fuels the car in order to wear out the tyres.

Suarez himself places some restriction on the use of the axiom when he says that the "per se" effect must be foreseen before it can be said to be directly willed in its cause. But if, in addition to the efficient agency of the cause, knowledge of the effect is demanded in order that the effect be ascribable to a human agent, why does he not require also that the effect be "propter finem", which is likewise a prerequisite of rational finality? The axiom "Qui vult causam vult effectum", has its true application and relevance only if the cause is willed as a "causa qua causa", that is to say, in view of its causal properties, for only then does its effects flow from the will in the manner proper to human acts (80).

3.3.2.2.2. The Salmanticenses

The Salmanticenses identify two classes of effects "per se". The first class is constituted by an unlawful effect that proceeds from a cause (per se) in such a manner that it is the sole immediate effect of the act and consequently all other effects flow through it. Where it is not the sole immediate effect, it is such that the desired effect flows through it. Regarding such an effect and its cause the Salmanticenses maintain:

> "We must say first that as often as some cause is so determined to an unlawful effect or motion that it either has no other effect, or it results in another effect, neither the cause nor the effect can be excused from sin". (81)

---

79 cf. Herbert G. Krammer, **The Indirect Voluntary or the Voluntarium in causa**, Washington 1935, p. 39.

80 See the Salmanticenses, op. cit., tr. 13, dis. 10, dub. 6, nn. 241-246.

81 ibid. n. 214.

It is analytically evident that the causing of the unlawful effects that fall under this class is always directly willed, since such effects are either the end of an action or the means to the desired end.

The second class of effect "per se" is constituted by an illicit (per se) effect which does not proceed from its cause as the sole immediate effect of the act of the will nor is it the means to the desired effect. Consequently, it is accompanied by a good effect which also proceeds immediately from the cause; or the unlawful effect is produced by means of the good effect. Regarding a "per se" effect and a cause which belongs to this class, the Salmanticenses declare:

> "Even though a cause results per se in some evil effect,
> it is lawful to actuate the cause of the evil effect, if a
> proportionate serious good effect follows equally immediate-
> ly from the cause or preceeds the evil effect. And although
> the evil effect may be foreseen, it may not be intended
> ..." (82)

The Salmanticenses argue that evil effects of this type could be produced without their being directly intended, that is to say, they could proceed from the will as indirectly willed effects. They maintain that the causation of such evil effects could be justified for a proportionate grave reason.

It is enlightening to note that an overriding number of catholic authors (83) share the opinion of the Salmanticenses. It is also instructive to observe that this teaching as well as their doctrine on the voluntary nature of "per accidens" effect which agrees with the position of Suarez are preserved in the catholic tradition in the doctrine of direct and indirect voluntariness which stands at the core of the traditional formulation of the principle of double effect. A few illustrations may help to highlight this point.

First, what the Salmanticenses classed as "per se" effect that is directly willed, namely, an unlawful "per se" effect that proceeds from its cause as the immediate effect of the act, is reflected in the description of direct killing by catholic moralists. For instance Regatillo and Zalba asserts:

----

82 ibid. n. 139.

83 Billuart, **Summa S. Thomae**, tr. de jure et justitia diss. 10, art. 5, n. 1; Dumas, op. cit. vol. 1, pp. 79-80; Genicot-Salsmans, **Institutiones Theologiae Moralis**, (Brussel 1927, 2 ed.) vol. 1, nn. 10, 14; Merkelbach, op. cit., vol. 1., n. 143, 4 b; Noldin, op. cit., vol. 1, n. 83 b.

"Occisio ... directa per actionem scl. quae immediate dirigitur ad destruendam vitam ... ex ipsa natura actionis bene perspecta, quae nullum alium effectum immediatum habet ..." (84)

The same formulation appears in the "Canadian Code of Ethical and Religious Directives for Catholic Hospitals" which states: "Any procedure whose sole immediate effect is the death of a human being is a direct killing" (85).

Second, effects "per se" classed by Salmanticenses as indirectly willed are mirrored by the condition of the principle of double effect which states that the good effect should proceed from the act at least as immediate as the evil.

Third, the demands made by the Salmanticenses that the evil effect may not be intended and that there must be a proportionate grave reason for permitting it are all reflected by the traditional formulation of the principle of double effect.

Fourth, the Salmanticenses maintain that the effects whether "per se" or "per accidens" describable as indirectly willed are restricted to illicit effects, that is to say, to intrinsic evil (effects). Similarly, catholic moral traditions restricts the application of the principle of double effect to conflict situations involving intrinsic evil.

Finally, it will be belabouring the obvious to say that by identifying a second group of "per se" effects indirectly willed and teleologically assessed, the Salmanticenses, whose stand is discernable in the traditional formulation of the principle of double effect, adopt a benign or mild interpretation of what otherwise would have been a strict or absolute prohibition of all "per se" evil effects as propounded by Suarez. Thanks to this restrictive interpretation of the prohibition of acts that produce "per se" evil effects (that is to say, to acts assessed deontologically), catholic tradition is able to solve many of the problems presented by conflict situations involving such acts while still paying, as it were, a lip service to its traditional doctrine of the deontological prohibition of such acts.

----

84 Regatillo-Zalba, op. cit., vol. 2, p. 280; see also Mausbach-Ermecke, op. cit., vol. 3, p. 243. Charles Curran points out that direct killing is "an action whose finis operis is killing. Catholic moralists have generally agreed that when the sole immediate effect of the action is killing the action is direct killing". Charles E. Curran, **Christian Morality**, (London 1969), p. 238.

85 cf. Gerald Kelly, **Medico-Moral Problems**, (St. Louis 1958), p. 56.

PART TWO

MODERN REINTERPRETATION OF THE PRINCIPLE OF DOUBLE EFFECT

Catholic Tradition, by employing the principle of double effect to the deontological norms, interpretes them restrictively and thereby tries to minimize the hardships that would have otherwise followed from a strict interpretation of these norms. Thus, for instance, in the classical case of an ectopic gestation, where mother and child would have perished if the deontological norms were strictly followed, tradition is, at least, able to save the life of the mother by permitting the indirect killing of the foetus. This represents a bold step towards dissolving the deontological norms into a teleological system. However, this step does not seem to resolve all the problems that arise from the deontological interpretation of moral norms by Tradition.

One of such problems is easily perceived by the further analysis of the application of the principle of double effect to the case of ectopic gestation. While the principle would allow the excision of the fallopian tube, it proscribes the shelling out of the foetus, a procedure which apparently causes lesser harm in comparison to the former which is considered the morally right act.

One may ask whether the principle of double effect, in proscribing the course of action that seemingly causes lesser harm than its prescribed alternative, does not contradict the preference principle. If the direct killing of the foetus is in itself a moral evil, then it does not contradict it, since one may not perform a morally evil act in order to achieve a non-moral good (the preservation of the woman's fertility). If this is the case, it reflects the preference principle which in this instance would demand that when a moral evil and a non-moral evil conflict with each other one must avoid the former, which is the greater evil. On the other hand, if the direct killing of an innocent person is to be proved to be only causing a non-moral disvalue, then the principle of double effect contradicts the preference principle, by permitting a course of action that causes loss of life as well as loss of fertility in preference to that which causes only loss of life.

Now Tradition appears to end the journey towards dissolving the deontological norms into a teleological system because it strongly believes that it has arrived at the borderline where deontological norms resolutely resist any further modification. This belief is sustained by the claim that the disvalues proscribed by the deontological norms are not non-moral disvalues but moral evils, which must always be avoided. Thus the question regarding whether the principle of double effect contradicts the preference principle or not rests ultimately on the reply to the question on whether Tradition is right or wrong in norming acts deontologically. How do the two modern authors chosen go about this question?

4.

PETER KNAUER'S REINTERPRETATION OF THE PRINCIPLE
OF DOUBLE EFFECT

Peter Knauer, the first to give a critical attention to the principle of double effect in recent times, attends to this rule in a series of writings (1). The thesis he propounds in these writings and the arguments he employs are basically the same. One notable difference consists in the fact that some issues are better elaborated in one writing than in the others. Thus, for the purposes of this work it would not be necessary to treat each of Knauer's articles separately. Also for the same reason it might not be necessary to repeat all his thesis. It suffices to state clearly how Knauer tries to reinterprete the principle of double effect and the argument he employs to sustain his reformulation of this rule.

The main steps he takes in this exercise include the following assertions:

a) that tradition identifies physical categories with moral ones;

b) that psychological intention and moral intention are two distinct and different realities;

c) that qualitatively different values are incomparable with each other.

These assertions and the arguments that support them will be exposed fully and examined critically in the succeeding pages.

---

1 Peter Knauer, "La détermination du bien et du mal moral par le principe du double effet", in: NRTh. 87 (1965), 365-76.
   - "The Hermeneutic Function of the Principle of Double Effect; in: Charles Curran and Richard McCormick eds., **Readings in Moral Theology No. 1**, New York 1979, pp. 1-39. This article appeared first in **Natural Law Forum**, 12 (1967), 132-162.

   - "Das rechtverstandene Prinzip von der Doppelwirkung als Grundnorm jeder Gewissensentscheidung", in: ThGl., 57 (1967), 107-133.

   - "Überlegungen zur moraltheologischen Prinzipienlehre der Enzyklika 'Humanae Vitae'", ThPh., 45 (1970), 60-74.

   - **Der Glaube kommt vom Hören - Ökumenische Fundamentaltheologie**, Graz 1978, 61-76.

   - "Fundamentalethik: Teleologische als deontologische Normenbegründung", in: ThPh., 55 (1980), 321-360.

4.1. EXPOSITION OF KNAUER'S ARGUMENTS

a) PHYSICAL CATEGORIES EQUATED WITH MORAL ONES IN TRADITION

Knauer asserts that in catholic moral teaching it is not seldom that moral categories are identified with physical ones (2). He instances the catholic teaching on "Fontes moralitatis" where, as he says, the "finis operis" of an act is equated to the external effect that could be photographed. He notes that the physical character of an act of killing a human being, for instance, does not differ in murder, self-defence or in the execution of a duly deserved capital punishment. Similarly, he observes that the physical character of an act of almsgiving does not differ from money exchanging hands in bribery, in payment of a debt, in lending money and so on. Were the physical character of an act to be identified with the "finis operis" or moral object, then these acts whose moral character are essentially different from each other would have one and the same moral object. If this cannot be deemed right the moral object must be sought elsewhere, namely, in the motive of the agent.

Furthermore, Knauer remarks that the error of equating physical categories with moral ones is manifested also in the traditional application of the principle of double effect. He notes that in applying the principle to the classic case of treating a pregnant woman who has a cancerous uterus, Tradition permits the excision of the uterus along with child in order to save the mother. On the other hand, where the uterus may still be healed, Tradition forbids the removal of the foetus alone, an alternative which causes lesser harm in as much as the woman's fertility is preserved. This procedure is deemed prohibited because it is considered direct killing of an innocent person. The killing of the foetus is the means to saving the woman's life and thus a contravention of the condition of the principle of double effect which requires that the evil effect should not be the means to obtaining the intended good.

Knauer objects to this manner of applying the principle and says that "When the categories of direct and indirect are confused with purely physical categories, a blind hair-splitting is introduced into ethics." (3)

----

2   Peter Knauer, "The Hermeneutic Function ...", p. 20.

3   ibid. p. 20.

b) MORAL INTENTION IS NOT EQUIVALENT TO PSYCHOLOGICAL INTENTION

Knauer seems to think that the principle of double effect proscribes the direct intention of the evil effect (the death of the foetus) because Tradition generally deems the intentional causation of physical or non-moral evil morally wrong. Since he is, at any rate, of this opinion himself and since he also believes that each ethical or moral evil embraces a non-moral evil in its constitution, he asserts that the traditional principle of double effect responds to the question: under what condition is the causation or permission of a non-moral evil morally permitted and when is it not (4)? In response to this question he declares in an unmistakable teleological tone that the causation or permission of a non-moral evil is a moral evil in every case where it is directly intended. Conversely, causing or permitting a non-moral evil is not a moral evil when it is indirectly intended.

Thus in his view the principle of double effect may be concisely formulated as follows: "One may permit the evil effect of his act if this is not intended in itself but is indirect and justified by a commensurate reason." (5) By reformulating the traditional principle of double effect in this manner Knauer strips it of the conditions requiring that the act should not be in itself intrinsically evil and that the good effect should not be produced by means of the evil, conditions that bear the hallmarks of a deontological thinking. Since his reformulation of the principle rotates around the axis of the notions of direct/indirect intention and proportionate reason, he finds it necessary to clarify what he takes these terms to mean.

In explaining the meaning of the direct/indirect intention he relies heavily and solely on St. Thomas' teaching on the killing of an unjust aggressor in the act of self-defence (S. Th. II-II, q. 64, a. 7). Relying on J.T. Mangan's thesis he believes that this text is the prestine application of the principle of double effect.

In this text Thomas teaches, among other things, that moral acts take their species according to what is intended and not according to what is beyond the intention (praeter intentionem). An act of self-defence has two effects, the saving of one's own life and the slaying of the aggressor. While the former is intended, the other is "praeter intentionem". Although an act of self-defence proceeds from the good intention of saving one's life, it may, however, be illicit because it is not proportionate to its end, that is, if one uses more force than is necessary to save one's life.

In his interpretation of this text Knauer remarks that although the death of the aggressor is a means towards the saving of the life of the assaulted, Thomas says that it is "praeter intentionem". The momentous question here is to show how in this case a physical means to an end is to be seen as unintended. In reply to this question

----

4 Peter Knauer, "Fundamentalethik ...", p. 234.

5 Peter Knauer, "The Hermeneutic Function ...", p. 5.

Knauer asserts that self-defence is morally directly intended and the death of the aggressor indirectly intended (praeter intentionem), if and only if the killing of the aggressor is the necessary or only means by which the assaulted can save his life. In this instance the killing of the aggressor, the non-moral evil, remains beyond the intention because there is a proportionate reason, namely, self-defence. If, on the other hand, the assaulted could save his life merely by disabling or mutilating the aggressor, then killing him in such a case would mean employing a means not proportionate to the end of self-defence. In such a case the death of the aggressor, the non-moral evil, is ethically directly intended.

Knauer deduces from this that the direct and indirect intention of non-moral evil can only be determined by the presence or absence of a proportionate reason. Intending a non-moral evil is direct if a proportionate reason is wanting, and indirect if there is a proportionate reason.

Redefining intention in this manner Knauer stresses that moral and psychological intentions are two distinct and different realities. To illustrate this new teaching, he adduces a couple of concrete examples. Two of these suffice to clarify this distinction.

1. In a medical operation a surgeon directs his attention towards the skillful excision of a diseased member. Usually Tradition employs the principle of totality to justify such a medical procedure. By appealing to this principle the excision of the diseased member, a non-moral evil, is understood as directly intended. Knauer objects to this. He says that the excision is merely psychologically intended as a means; it remains, however, beyond the moral intention in as much as there is a corresponding grave reason for the medical procedure. By foregoing such an operation the life of the patient will be endangered and thus the continued possession of the sick member will be rendered impossible. It will be contrary to reason or "contra naturam" in a moral sense if in this situation one wants to retain the sick member. On the other hand, if a medical operation is not justifiable in this manner, then the case is no longer a healing operation but a case of a proscribed mutilation. The resulting non-moral evil is morally intended in such a case (6).

2. In stealing a thief psychologically intends only his personal enrichment. He hardly thinks of, nor psychologically intends, the resulting harm done to his victim, who is dispossessed. Morally considered, however, the material damage (non-moral evil) done to his victim is directly intended, since each non-moral evil is morally directly intended whose causation or permission is not justified by a proportionate reason (7).

In the first example the non-moral evil of the excision of a sick member of the body is psychologically intended but morally indirectly intended because there is a corresponding grave reason. In the second example the material damage inflicted on the dispossessed man is not

----

6   Peter Knauer, "Überlegungen ...", pp. 64-65.

7   ibid.

psychologically intended but it is, nevertheless, morally intended because a proportionate reason for causing such a non-moral evil (loss
of property) is wanting. By employing these contrasting examples
Knauer tries to demonstrate that whether a non-moral evil is psychologically intended or not plays no role in determining a moral intention. A moral intention is established only by the presence or absence
of a proportionate reason.

Above and beyond, Knauer maintains that the direct/indirect moral intention of non-moral evil understood rightly as causing or permitting a non-moral evil without or with a proportionate reason is the
key to understanding the different tracts of catholic moral theology.
Failure to reflect deeply enough on this distinction led catholic moralists of the past to multiplying names referring to these two simple
realities and, as it were, contravened Ockham's dictum: "entia non
sunt multiplicanda sine necessitate." In Knauer's opinion, for example, for want of a proportionate reason material cooperation becomes
formal cooperation; extrinsic evil becomes intrinsic evil; the binding
force of Affirmative Laws which is said to be "semper, sed non pro
semper" turns to "semper et pro semper" of the Negative Precepts.

c)   CLARIFICATION OF PROPORTIONATE REASON

It is evident from the foregoing exposition that basic to Knauer's
reformulation of the principle of double effect is the decisive role
played by proportionate reason in the moral evaluation of an action.
If a proportionate reason is lacking the causation or permission of a
non-moral evil is directly intended and so immoral; if there is a proportionate reason it is indirectly intended and so morally allowed.
What does Knauer take proportionate reason to mean?

In clarifying his understanding of proportionate reason, Knauer
first and foremost expresses utter dissatisfaction over its traditional
formulation within the ambient of the principle of double effect as:
the good achieved must, at least, correspond to the evil accepted in
exchange or outweigh it. His discontent is motivated by two reasons
(8). First, such a formulation, he says, leads to ethical rigorism.
One is no longer left with the alternatives of choosing between acting
in either a good or a better way; he who fails to act in the better
way acts morally wrongly. Second and more important, such a formulation involves a quantitative comparison of values which are qualitatively different and consequently cannot be compared with one another. Knauer asks sneeringly how he who is faced with the alternatives of studying medicine or music can judge which of the two qualitatively different values is the greater.

Thus in his view the relevant ethical question here is not: which
good among the different goods open to one's choice is one to decide

----

8   Peter Knauer, "Fundamentalethik ...", p. 328.

for? Rather the question regards the way and manner one is to strive after the good for which one has decided (9). In replying to the latter question Knauer remarks that in every act a person strives either to achieve a value or to avoid a disvalue. To achieve either of these objectives he has to pay a price, that is to say, he has to cause or tolerate a disvalue. Consequently, in every human act a harm or disvalue is caused or tolerated. This harm could be proportionate to the value sought or it could undermine it.

When is the harm caused proportionate to the value sought? Or stating this question in different words, when is there a proportionate reason? A proportionate reason is at hand, according to Knauer, if and only if the physical evil caused or permitted does not in the long run and on the whole (auf die Dauer und im ganzen) undermine the good sought. He who acts out of a proportionate reason promotes the good sought in a universal sense or absolutely, apart from any reference to the specific persons or community of persons for whom it is concretly enhanced.

In contrast, an act which lacks proportionate reason is counter-productive. "A good is sought while the conditions for the highest possible realization of the good are abandoned." (10) A student may like to acquire as much knowledge as possible. To achieve his objective he has to interrupt his studies from time to time. Should he be bent only on his studies at the detriment of his health, he may, for a short time, achieve something above average but the result on the whole and in the long run will be much under average. He may even, in an extreme case, become sick and so achieve nothing. By forebearing to take rest — a means necessary for the achievement of his end on the whole and in the long run — the student seeks an objective which has an appropriate price at all costs. He thereby acts unintelligently and thus immorally.

In sum Knauer believes that the traditional principle of double effect is the fundamental principle of normative ethics which responds to the question regarding when it is morally right to cause or permit a non-moral evil. It is morally right, he says, to cause or permit a non-moral evil when it is indirectly intended. To be indirectly intended there must be a proportionate reason for causing or tolerating it. And there is a proportionate reason when the means or the non-moral evil caused or tolerated does not on the whole and in the long run undermine the good sought.

---

9   ibid.

10 Peter Knauer, "The Hermeneutic Function ...", p. 13.

4.2. APPRECIATION OF KNAUER'S REINTERPRETATION OF THE PRINCIPLE OF DOUBLE EFFECT

William Conway (11), in his discussion of the principle of double effect in his article of 1951, writes:

"To many students of theology there is something vaguely dissatisfying about the teaching of moralists on the "act of two effects" ... there is the question of intention, which at times seems to bedevil the whole problem."

These words indicate, among other things, that the principle of double effect posed problems also to the moralists of the past. In attending to these problems these moralists, in general, tried to preserve as much as possible the "inviolability" of the deontological norms and also preserve thereby the moral cul-de-sac which these norms sometimes create.

Knauer, by trying as it were to find a way out of the blind alley, forebears interpreting deontologically the norms guiding the acts that fall within the scope of the principle of double effect. By making such a move he embraces a teleological methodology of grounding ethical norms. This attempt is evidently a bold breaking of new grounds in the catholic moral tradition, which speaks to the credit of the highly talented intellect that conceived it. A reader strongly tends to doffing his hat in admiration of this rare performance when he recalls that Knauer conceived this idea while still only a student. The importance of this work can be seen in the amount of influence it has made on many contemporary catholic moralists who have adopted a teleological method of interpreting ethical norms and also how frequently it is quoted (12).

When Knauer first published his thesis in 1965 the doing of normative ethics was not directly undertaken by catholic moralists within

---

11 William Conway, "The Act of Two Effects", in: Irish Theological Quarterly, 18 (1951), 125.

12 Knauer outlines a catalogue of modern authors who have had reasons to recourse to his thesis in footnote 5 of his "Fundamentalethik ...", p. 322.

the framework of fundamental moral theology (13). This is not because these moralists were not familiar with the problems of normative ethics but probably because they did not draw a clear-cut distinction between normative ethics and metaethics. However, in recent times this distinction has been drawn by catholic moralists and they have been carrying on a lot of research in the field of normative ethics. With the light gained from the results of these efforts, one stands today in a considerably good stead to detect the limitations of Knauer's work. For the purposes of appreciating the limitations better they will be considered under the following headings:

a) An unrestricted application of the principle of double effect.

b) Physical categories should not be equated with moral categories.

c) Psychological intention is not equivalent to moral intention.

d) Incomparability of qualitatively different values.

4.2.1. AN UNRESTRICTED APPLICATION OF THE PRINCIPLE

After examining Knauer's treatment of the principle of double effect Germain Grisez concludes that "Knauer is carrying through a revolution in principle while pretending only a clarification." (14) The truth of this statement is partly evident when the restricted application of the principle by Tradition is contrasted with Knauer's unrestricted application of the rule to every act.

Tradition, as it has been indicated in the first section of this work, knows two types of evil and good producing acts, should acts be judged from the character of the evil they produce. The first

---

13 cf. B. Schüller: Various Types of Grounding for Ethical Norms", in: Charles Curran/R.A. McCormick, eds. **Readings in Moral Theology No. 1**, p. 189: "In the handbooks of fundamental moral theology one will look in vain for a tract that deals directly with what is called 'normative ethics' today. Tradition occupies itself with the question as to what constitutes the standard of ethical behavior: right reason or human nature. But no matter which way that question is resolved, in special ethics all argue the same way. Tradition is concerned with clarifying what is meant by "natural moral law" or "natural law". In so doing, however, it tackles questions which only indirectly concern a normative ethics; e. g., the objectivity of ethical value-judgements, the relationship of axiology and ontology, the distinction between phýsei dikaion and thései dikaion, and the relationship between an ethics of reason and an ethics of faith."

14 Germain Grisez, **Abortion**: The Myths, the Realities, and the Arguments, New York 1970, p. 331.

110

group of acts are good and non-moral evil producing. These are usually normed teleologically. Since for a proportionate reason a non-moral evil may be intended as "bonum utile", Tradition does not find it meaningful to apply the direct/indirect distinction to such acts. The second group of acts are good and intrinsic (moral) evil producing. Tradition usually applies the principle of double effect only to these acts. Since forebearing to cause or tolerate an intrinsic evil may in certain situations lead to intolerable hardships, Tradition permits its causation by applying the principle and insisting thereby that the intrinsic (moral) evil should not be directly intended.

In sharp contrast, Knauer, by his reinterpretation of the principle of double effect extends the rule to the evaluation of every act. Thus out of a rule which is employed as a particular principle by Tradition, Knauer creates a universal principle. He accomplishes this by bringing intrinsic and non-moral evils to a common denominator of non-moral evils.

It might be asked whether Knauer is justified in reducing intrinsic (moral) evil to non-moral evil in the way he does. Perhaps why one is unable to answer this question with an unqualified "yes" or an unqualified "no" is because it is a question containing many questions. This complex question encapsules, at least, the question regarding whether the way and manner he carries out the transformation exercise is justifiable.

How does he do it? Knauer subsumes every intrinsic (moral) evil into the category of non-moral evil by creating a new criterion for establishing a moral evil based on a teleological logic. A moral evil, he declares, consists in the last analysis in the permission or causing of a non-moral evil which is not justified by a commensurate reason. By this, he implies that to establish the moral wrongness of every act the disvalues resulting from it must be subjected to teleological assessment. Thus he argues implicitly that Tradition is wrong in assessing intrinsic (moral) evil acts deontologically.

Has Knauer thus succeeeded in proving that Tradition is wrong in interpreting ethical norms detonologically? He can scarcely be said to have done so. Putting it in practical terms all he has done tantamounts to saying: "Tradition, your are wrong and I am right". The most appropriate and perhaps the only means of proving Tradition wrong is by critically examining the arguments it employs in supporting its deontological norms and showing that they are logically inconclusive. One who intends to build a new house on an old site has first to level down the existing building. New wine is not poured into old wine skin!

Knauer's tendency of failing to examine the reasons advanced by Tradition in bolstering its teachings is also evident in his claiming that the direct/indirect intention of physical evil understood respectively as the absence or presence of proportionate reason is equivalent to the textbook teaching on formal/material cooperation, intrinsic/extrinsic evil and so on. A nodding acquaintance with the traditional presentation of these tracts shows, for instance, that the principle of classification of evil into intrinsic and extrinsic has nothing to do with the absence or presence of proportionate reason.

The distinction between intrinsic and extrinsic evil is understand-able only within the context of the traditional teaching on intrinsic and extrinsic morality. Here some acts, namely, the intrinsically evil acts are said to be forbidden because they are in themselves evil. Others, namely, the extrinsically evil acts are said to be evil be-cause they are prohibited. Acts which fall within the class of the ex-trinsic morality depend on the positive precept for their morality, while acts belonging to the intrinsic morality are good or evil in them-selves according to their correspondence to or contradiction of the moral law. Failing to get at the grassroots of the traditional teaching on such divisions Knauer takes an illigitimate leap to conclude that all of them correspond to his reinterpreted version of the direct/in-direct intention.

If one were to ignore the shortcomings in the move Knauer takes in subsuming intrinsic evil into the class of non-moral evil and as-sume that he is right in doing so, the logical inference to be drawn from this would be that the principle of double effect, with its direct/indirect distinction is redundant, since one may directly intend a non-moral evil for a proportionate reason. Evidently Knauer would frown at such a deduction by retorting that the direct intention of a non-moral evil without a moral default is only imaginable to one who has not as yet learnt to distinguish between a psychological and a moral intention.

At the root of this distinction lies Knauer's belief that Tradition confuses moral categories with physical ones. Thus the necessity or appropriateness of this distinction partially rests on the truth of this belief. To what extent is this belief true?

4.2.2. PHYSICAL CATEGORIES SHOULD NOT BE EQUATED WITH MORAL CATEGORIES

Dominicus Prümmer echoes part of the teaching of catholic moral tradition on human acts when he says: "In omni actu humano distin-gui potest duplex esse: physicum et morale" (15). By this he indicates in unequivocal terms that in catholic moral tradition "esse physicum" is not "esse morale" and "esse morale" is not "esse physicum". The two are usually seen as two distinct and different realities.

It therefore comes as a surprise to read from Knauer in his treat-ment of "fontes moralitatis" and in his analysis of the traditional application of the principle of double effect that catholic tradition

----

15 Dominicus Prümmer, **Manuale Theologiae Moralis**, vol. I, no. 99, p. 67. See also Regatillo-Zalba, op. cit. vol. 1, p. 150.

confuses moral categories with physical (16). Richard McCormick disagrees with Knauer on this issue. Among other things he objects to Knauer's insistence that the "finis operis" must incorporate proportionate reason. He believes that Knauer has failed to distinguish the various meanings of proportionate reason.

"Proportionate reason can mean two things. Some proportionate reason are identical with the good effect as produced immediately by the cause (or with the cause as producing this effect as one equally immediate with several others). Other proportionate reasons are as motives "introduced from outside" so to speak, and superimposed on an external act whose basic meaning is already determined (because of its unique immediate effect)" (17).

It is evident from McCormick's remark that the weakness of Knauer's criticism on the "fontes moralitatis" springs from his failure to distinguish here between the moral rightness or wrongness of the action performed by a person and the moral goodness or badness of his motives.

In considering the "fontes moralitatis" it is necessary to bear in mind that when Tradition describes an action in this tract as good or bad, as right or wrong, as praiseworthy or blameworthy it is already presumed that it is a free deliberate act, since only such acts have

----

16 Apparently Knauer is not alone in making this claim. William van der Marck, in his works: **Love and Fertility**, London 1965, and **Towards a Christian Ethic**, New York 1967, levelled a similar criticism against the catholic tradition. In addition, it has become a fashion for many anglo-american moralists who treat the principle of double effect or discuss the problems of medical ethics to accuse this tradition of "physicalism" and consequently to take it to task. To what extent is this attack justifiable?
Schüller attempts to reply to this question by attending to the objections of van der Marck. In a word van der Marck is of the opinion that Tradition wrongly considers biochemical reaction, muscular movements, killing, removal of something belonging to another and so on as subjects of moral predicates: 'good' and 'evil'. He stresses that the intersubjective dimensions of these acts must be brought into consideration before they qualify as candidates of moral judgment. In attending to van der Marck's argument, Schüller points out that no evidence can be brought forward to show that Tradition ever considers muscular movements and biochemical reactions as subjects of moral judgment, since each of them is an "actus humani". On the other hand, killing and 'removing something from another' are subjects of moral judgment in so far as they are deliberate acts. Cf. Schüller, "Neuere Beiträge ...", pp. 135-138.

17 Richard McCormick, **Notes on Moral Theology 1965 Through 1980**, Washington D.C. 1981, p. 4.

a claim to such descriptions. In isolation from the motives or intention of the agent who performs it, a deliberate act can be rightly subjected to moral assessment. Put in different words, without considering whether the motive of an agent is good or bad, one can ask whether the act performed is morally right or wrong. Without considering whether Mr A who deliberately and freely gives money to the poor does so with the ulterior motive of improving his reputation or not, one can appraise the moral rightness or wrongness of the act of deliberately giving money to the poor.

The claim that the character of a unit of action like giving of alms cannot be determined in isolation from the motive of the agent is contestible. The concrete situation determines the meaning of an action. The motives of he who gives money (to the needy) need not be considered in order to establish whether this is paying a debt or giving relief to a poor man whom the donor owes nothing and from whom he expects no favour. Mr A's act can be assessed as morally right, even though his self-seeking motive is morally reproachable.

During the sermon on the mount Christ makes it clear that a deliberate act could be assessed positively irrespective of the self-seeking motives of the doer when he says: "Be careful not to parade your good deeds before men to attract their notice" (MT. 6:1). In this text "good deeds" or "work of righteousness", fasting, praying and almsgiving, are understandable as morally right acts independent of the donor's motive of attracting attention which is morally bad.

Now what is to be said about Knauer's assertion that Tradition confuses physical categories with moral ones because the principle of double effect demands that the evil effect should not preceed the good?

In attending to this question it is appropriate to remark that a moralist, in doing normative ethics, does not only concern himself with the rightness or wrongness of human actions but also with the reasons advanced in support of the assertion that an act is right or wrong. Knauer, in examining the classical application of the principle of double effect to the case of a pregnant woman with a diseased uterus interests himself in the fact that Tradition says it is morally wrong for the good effect to proceed from the death of the foetus as means. He fails to examine the reasons why Tradition considers it morally wrong. Failing to make this inquiry he by-passes the crux of the problem with which the principle of double effect is concerned, namely, the problem posed by norming acts deontologically and the related question regarding how right Tradition is in doing so.

Assuming that by judging the act of killing of a foetus deontologically Tradition is right to say that it is morally wrong because it is performed "ex defectu juris in agente", then Knauer can not reasonably object to the condition of the principle which requires that the healing of the woman should not proceed from the killing of the foetus. Here would be an instance where the maxim: "The good end does not sanctify the (morally) evil means" is morally binding. If, on the other hand, Tradition is wrong in judging this act morally evil with the deontological reasoning it employs, then it is incumbent on Knauer to prove it wrong. In a logical disputation error is not presumed; it is proved.

Knauer, by forebearing to inquire into the reason Tradition offers for considering intending to kill the foetus as a means to healing the woman morally wrong, and also by failing to note that Tradition considers the killing of an innocent person an intrinsic (moral) evil, presumes that Tradition sees it as the causing of a non-moral evil as he does. This is a fatal misinterpretation of Tradition, if Knauer makes this presumption.

Killing in a just war is an excellent example to elucidate what Tradition considers moral evil and non-moral evil and its different prescription towards intending or tolerating them. A pilot bombing installations in an area densely populated by non combatants, foresees that he will kill combatants as well as non-combatants. While Tradition permits his intending to kill the combatants, it proscribes the intention to kill the non-combatants. What explains this double standard in the moral evaluation of the intentional attitude of the same man towards the same act which destroys exactly the same values – human lives? The reason is that the killing of combatants is assessed teleologically; the causation of the death of the combatants is justifiable for a proportionate reason. In this context proportionate reason is explained in terms of the principle of "moderamem inculpatae tutelae": in self defence a nation may use moderate or appropriate force to ward-off the unjust aggression of its enemies even if it is foreseen to result in the death of the latter. Since the causation of the death of the combatants (non-moral disvalue) is a necessary means to warding-off aggression, it may be intended as a "bonum utile".

In contrast, the killing of non-combatants is usually judged deontologically and seen as the causing of an intrinsic or moral evil. When a moral evil must be caused in the course of achieving a proportionate good the principle of double effect insists that it must never be intended for obvious reasons. Moral evil "ex definitione" falls outside the range of what can be legitimately intended.

Knauer, perhaps, learns from the verbal formulation of the principle of double effect that the evil effect should not be intended and extends this principle, without discrimination, to every species of evil. Since, however, in every day life non-moral evil is employed as a means to achieving a good and consequently (psychologically) necessarily intended, Knauer finds it necessary to show that moral intention differs from psychological intention. Does he succeed in justifying this distinction?

4.2.3. PSYCHOLOGICAL INTENTION IS NOT EQUIVALENT TO MORAL INTENTION

Knauer believes that he can find justification for his reinterpretation of the traditional meaning of the direct/indirect intention by appealing to St. Thomas' teaching on self-defence against an unjust aggressor in Summa Theologica II,II, q. 64, a. 7. In this regard he claims that the origin of the principle is traceable to this text. The only evidence he adduces to back up this claim is that John Mangan makes this assertion.

As can be recalled the question of tracing the origin of the principle of double effect to St Thomas' teaching on self-defence is a highly controverted issue. The controverted nature of this question makes the text inadequate to serve the purpose of demonstrating the origin of the principle. In reply to Knauer's claim, for instance, one could simply assert that the origin of the principle is not traceable to this text because J. Ghoos is of this view. With such a counter-claim every argument will grind to a halt or at least will be suspended till a more compelling evidence is offered. However, for the purposes of carrying forth this argument, Knauer will be given the benefit of the doubt.

Assuming that the principle of double effect is traceable to this text, does Knauer validly justify his remodelled understanding of the direct/indirect intention from it? Does this text distinguish between psychological and moral intention as Knauer does? Does anything in the text show that Thomas, for instance, understands indirect intention as causing or permitting a physical evil with a proportionate reason?

In discussing the killing of human beings, Thomas distinguishes between the killing of innocent persons and evil doers (homines peccatores, malefactores) (18). Regarding the former he declares "nullo modo licet occidere innocentem" (19). In respect to killing an evildoer he distinguishes further between killing by a **public authority** (publica auctoritate) and by **private persons** (privatae personae) (20). Arguing in a teleological tone he asserts that if the welfare of the entire society demands it, a legitimately constituted public authority may slay a dangerous criminal. In sharp contrast to Knauer's view, Thomas states that a public authority may intend the death of the criminal (21). Thus in Thomas' view a non-moral evil may be intended for a proportionate reason.

---

18 cf. S. Th., II,II, q. 64, a. 2 - a. 4, and a. 6.

19 S. Th., II,II, q. 64, a. 6.

20 S. Th., II, II, q. 64, a. 3 and a. 7.

21 ibid.

While Thomas deems it permitted for a public authority to kill evil-doers he considers it forbidden for private persons to do so (22). To back this view he quotes the words of St Augustine: "A man who, without exercising public authority, kills an evil-doer, shall be judged guilty of murder". Thus in Thomas' opinion while the killing of a criminal by public authorities is the causing of a non moral evil performing the same act by private persons is considered a moral evil. Thus while he considers it a moral obligation for a public authority to intend killing a criminal when the common weal requires it, he deems it prohibited for private persons to intend to do so even in the process of self-defence (23).

That the killing of unjust aggressors in self-defence is the causing of a moral disvalue in the eyes of St Thomas helps his readers to understand that the class of evil he is referring to in Summa Theologica II, II, q. 64, a. 7 when he insists that evil should be "praeter intentionem" or "accidental" is not non-moral but moral evil. As if forestalling possible misinterpretations he makes reference to two passages: S. Th., I, II, q. 72, a. 1 and S. Th., II, II, q. 43, a. 3 where he employs similar terms specifically in dealing with moral evil. In the first he speaks of evil in the context of sin (a moral disvalue). In the second he employs the same terminology in reference to scandal (a moral disvalue). Here he says:

> "Scandal is accidental when it is beyond the agent's intention, as when a man does not intend, by his inordinate deed or word, to occasion another's downfall, but merely to satisfy his own will."

In contrast, when Thomas discusses the causation of evil understood as non-moral disvalue he does not demand that the evil should be "praeter intentionem" or "accidental". One can, for instance, recall that when he discusses the moral rightness of killing of plants and animals for food in S. Th., II, II, q. 64, a. 1 or the removal of other people's property by someone in an urgent need in S. Th., q. 66, a. 8 he does not employ such terms. For he does not find it meaningful to say that the ensuring non-moral evil should be "praeter intentionem".

----

22 S. Th., II, II, q. 64, a. 3 "it is lawful to kill an evildoer in so far as it is directed to the welfare of the whole community, so that it belongs to him alone who has charge of the community's welfare ... Now the care of the common good is entrusted to persons of rank having public authority: wherefore they alone, and not private individuals, can lawfully put evildoers to death".
Making the same point Thomas says in S. Th., q. 64, a. 7 "But as it is unlawful to take a man's life, except for the common good, as stated above (a. 3), it is not lawful for a man to intend killing a man in self-defence, except for such as have public authority, who while intending to kill a man in self-defence, refer this to the public good ...".

23 ibid.

How irreconcilable Knauer's view on intention in general and on the intention of evil in particular is with Thomas' opinion is vividly seen in the latter's teaching on God's willing of evil. He says that God

"in no way wills the evil of sin, which is the privation of the right order towards the divine good. The evil of natural defect or punishment He does will, by willing the good to which such evils are attached. Thus in willing justice He wills punishment and in willing the preservation of the natural order, He wills some things to be naturally corrupt." (24)

From the foregoing it is abundantly clear that Thomas' use of "praeter intentionem" is different from Knauer's use of indirect intention. While Thomas restricts the use of "praeter intentionem" or its equivalent to cases where he wants to indicate that moral disvalues should not be intended, Knauer employs indirect intention in insisting that non-moral evil should not be intended. In addition, while Thomas is of the opinion that non-moral evil could at times be willed as a means to achieving a good end, Knauer maintains that the intention of a non-moral evil is always morally wrong.

A further difference obtains in Knauer's and Thomas' views regarding the role played by proportionate reason in determining intention. In Knauer's view proportionate reason enters into the constitution of direct/indirect intention. Evidently Thomas is not of this opinion. This fact is apparent in the sequence of his argument in the Summa Theologica II, II, q. 64, a. 7, the very text cited by Knauer in defence of his view. Thomas argues that an act of self-defence may have two effects: the saving of one's own life and the slaying of the unjust aggressor's life. While the former is intended the other remains "praeter intentionem". Although the saving of one's life is the only effect intended and ipso facto the slaying of the life of the aggressor remains "praeter intentionem", the act may, nevertheless, be morally wrong, if more force is employed than is necessary to save one's life. In this case one can no longer be simply considered as merely intending to defend oneself. One may rather be seen as intending to take revenge. It may be worthwhile to point out that the question regarding the employment of more force than is necessary for self-defence is rather academic. In the process of self-defence it can be hardly imagined that a man is able to measure the amount of force he is using or what amount of force is necessary to stop the aggression of his attacker.

From the run of Thomas's argument what is intended and what is "praeter intentionem" are already determined by the posture of the will towards good and moral evil respectively before he sets forth to speak of the role played by proportionate reason. In a word, Thomas is simply saying that for the moral justification of the causation of moral evil it is not sufficient that the moral evil should not be intended but also there should be a proportionate reason for causing it.

---

24 S. Th., I, q. 19, a. 9.

It will, therefore, be belabouring the obvious to stress that St Thomas in his discussion on self-defence, does not subsume proportionate reason into the notion of intention as Knauer does.

It could be argued that although Knauer is wrong in seeking justification for his redefined notion of moral intention in Thomas' text on self-defence, this error does not, nevertheless, erase the truth of the point he is making regarding the necessity of distinguishes between psychological and moral intention in the way he does. Accordingly, it is worthwhile, if not mandatory, to test the truth of Knauer's claim.

Supposing in the execution of a capital punishment in a secluded area strictly reserved for this purpose, a soldier deliberately fires a series of bullets at a justly condemned criminal and kills him. At the same time a straying bullet from his rifle hits and kills an innocent by-passer. The soldier, by bringing about the death of the two, causes a physical or non-moral evil in each case. If these causations of two equal physical evils by the same person through the same process of shooting are to have different moral assessment it must be on account of some differences existing between the character of the actions. Now the differences consist in the following:

1) The soldier has a proportionate reason for executing the duly condemned criminal while he has none for the killing of the innocent by-passer.

2) The soldier directs his mind towards executing the condemned criminal but does not direct the same towards killing the innocent by-passer.

Were one to assess the acts morally solely by the facts contained in (1), one would, following Knauer's redefined (moral) intention, conclude that:

a) The soldier, in so far as he has a proportionate reason for carrying out the execution, does not intend the physical evil resulting from the death of the criminal. Therefore his causation of physical evil, being unintended, in this case is not morally wrong.

b) The soldier, in so far as he lacks proportionate reason in the killing of the by-passer, intends the resulting evil. Thus the causation of physical evil, being intended in this case, is morally wrong. Therefore the soldier is answerable for murder.

It is clear that although Knauer will accept conclusion (a) he will reject conclusion (b). Will he be consistent if he does so? Why would he reject (b)? He might argue that, even though the soldier deliberately released the shots, he did not deliberately aim at killing the innocent by-passer. Thus even though he is the physical cause of death of the by-passer, he is not its moral cause. If Knauer argues this way, as would be expected, he will be affirming what he denies. He would accept that psychological (deliberate) intention plays a morally significant role.

From this analysis it is evident that apart from the considerations of lack of proportionate reason the deliberate aiming at causing a non-moral disvalue by the mind plays a significant moral role in the moral assessment of an action. This deliberate-aiming-at an object by the mind, which is traditionally called intention, plays a moral significant role different from the role played by proportionate reason, which is the core of Knauer's redefined moral intention. Since these are two distinct and different realities, is there any use designating them with one name? Far from serving a useful purpose such a homonym will merely lead to confusion.

It is little wonder then why many able moralists refuse to endorse Knauer's redefined intention. For instance, Schüller (25) notes that this is superfluos and unnecessarily misleading. To expose its superfluity he applies it to a case of the execution of a capital punishment. If keeping to the sense of intention in common parlance a person were to ask the conditions for the moral justification of an intentional causation of a non-moral evil, he would receive the reply that this is the case when there is a proportionate reason. From this it could be concluded that he who carries out a just punishment against a condemned criminal may intend inflicting the non-moral evil because this is an infliction of a just punishment.

The foregoing analysis has shown that the distinction between psychological and moral intention can neither be justified by Thomas' teaching on self-defence nor can be seen as serving any useful purpose. To avoid the confusion it might bring about, it might be advisable to discard it.

4.2.4. INCOMPARABILITY OF QUALITATIVELY DIFFERENT VALUES

Why Knauer could come up with an objection against the traditional understanding of the proportionate reason in the way he does is perhaps best explained in the words of Ludwig Wittgenstein:

> "The aspect of things that are most important for us are hidden, because of their simplicity and familiarity. (One is unable to notice something – because it is always before one's eyes)" (26).

Perhaps because of their commonplace Knauer no longer seems to be aware of the fact that in their daily behaviour men consider and treat values as realities that are hierarchically structured as well as realities that can be estimated in material or quantitative terms. A couple of examples taken from every day experience may be helpful to bring this fact into clear view.

Catholics are bound to attend mass on Sundays and Holy Days of Obligation. Generally moralists teach that there are some "causae

---

25 Bruno Schüller, "Neuere Beiträge ...", p. 158.

26 Ludwig Wittgenstein, **Philosophical Investigation**, tr. G.E.M. Anscombe, Oxford Basil Blackwell 1953, 129.

excusantes" to this obligation. Excused from it are those with sufficient grave reason such as a disproportionately grave hardship. A
long distance from the church which takes a healthy person about 75
minutes to cover is generally considered as constituting such a disproportionately grave hardship. A person may ask axiological philosophers how the spiritual wealth of participating at mass is measured
against a 75 minutes walk. But could he object to this "causa ex-
cusans" simply because it involves an attempt at measuring things
that are qualitatively different from each other?

A man may be willing to pay a gate-free of 10 dollars to watch
a concert if Mr X, a renowned artist, is conducting the display but
not if Mr Y. This is because he is of the opinion that Mr X's performance is worth 10 dollars while Mr Y's is worth less than this amount.
Somebody may inquire from axiologists how the performance of a con-
ductor is measurable in monetary terms. But could he rightly reproach
the man in question for trying to compare things qualitatively different from each other?

Similarly a moment's reflection also shows that many received doc-
trines are erected on the belief that there is a hierarchy of values.
The teaching on the "summum bonum", for instance, presumes that values are hierarchically structured. God is thought of as the "summum
bonum" that is capable of satisfying man's infinite desire for happiness. Asserting that a "summum bonum" exists, of course, means that
it is taken for granted that goods are comparable with God, who, as
Creator, is qualitatively different from creatures. The hierarchy of disvalues is also presumed in the teaching on "advising the lesser of
two evils". Generally moralists teach that although it is unlawful to
induce another into committing a lesser sin, it is a holy thing to advise him who is already determined to commit a grave sin to commit
a lesser one in the same species instead. If sins (disvalues) are seen
in terms of "grave" and "lesser", it means they are being considered
comparatively.

In the same way the principle of double effect presumes the com-
parability of all values and disvalues when it asserts that the evil
caused must not be greater than the good achieved. Thus, while the
principle would permit a medically indicated abortion, that is to say,
abortion to save life, it prohibits an ethically indicated abortion,
that is to say, abortion to save face. This is because human life is
taken to be greater in value that honour.

Knauer objects to this traditional way of formulating the condition of proportionate reason within the framework of the principle
of double effect, because, as he says, it involves a quantitative comparison of values qualitatively different and so incomparable with one
another. It is evident that this claim stands diametrically opposed to
the presuppositions of everyday life and of many accepted teachings,
as has been indicated above.

These presuppositions find support in the teachings of some fairly
well known philosophers of value. For instance Hastings Rashdall says:

"It is to my mind a perfectly clear deliverance of the moral consciousness, that no action can be right except in so far as it tends to produce a good, and that, when we have to choose between goods, it is always right to choose the greater good. Such a doctrine implies that goods of all kinds can be compared, that we can place goods of all kinds in a single scale, and assign to each its value relatively to the rest ... But when circumstances make it impossible for me to secure for myself or for other all these kinds of good, then I can and must decide which of them I regard as best worth having; and that implies that for the purpose of choosing between them they are commensurable." (27)

Making the same point Ralf Barton Perry asserts:

"Such terms as 'better' and 'best', 'worse' and 'worst', 'higher' and 'lower', ... clearly imply 'more' and 'most', 'less' and 'least', in some sense. Many philosophers, having discovered that certain familiar principles of comparative magnitude which are applicable in arithmetic and physics are not applicable to values, have been content to dismiss the matter by simply denying that value is 'quantitative'. Meanwhile these philosophers themselves, in agreement with common sense, continue to employ a vocabulary which means comparative magnitude if it means anything. It does not much matter whether that which is quantitative in a qualified sense is called 'quantitative', or 'qualitative'; but it is highly important to discover precisely what it is, and how it justifies the use of at least some of the terms of the quantitative vocabulary, such as 'more' and 'less'. It appears to be the case, for example, that one value is greater than another in the sense that some terms lie beyond other terms in a serial order, and also in the sense that a whole exceeds any one of the parts which compose it." (28)

These passages hardly need further commentary other than saying that they show that Knauer's view has been propounded in the past as well as refuted.

It is remarkable to note that Knauer himself can scarcely abstain from comparing qualitatively different values when he discusses the morally wrong act. He says that an act is morally wrong when an "objective is sought which has an appropriate price (tantum – quantum), but sought at any price." (29) He illustrates this with a stu-

----

27 Hasting Rashdall, **The Theory of Good and Evil**, London 2 ed. 1924, pp. 38-39.

28 Ralph Barton Perry, **General Theory of Value**, Cambridge 1967, pp. 626-627.

29 Peter Knauer, "The Hermeneutic Function ...", p. 12.

dent who wants knowledge as an end and who, in achieving this objective, has to pay the commensurate price of studying and resting. Now analysing the process of studying, one finds that it involves reading, concentrating, reflecting and so on, processes which sap physical and mental energy. It is evident that before beginning his studies, Knauer's student was faced with the challenge of choosing between two mutually exclusive and qualitatively different values: conservation of physical and mental energy, on the one hand, and the acquisition of knowledge, on the other hand. By choosing one of the two alternatives the student gives preference to it; he compares the pros and cons of the two and chooses what in the given circumstances he considers the better alternative.

Experience teaches that life is full of situations where values conflict with one another. Such situations pose perplexing problems to a person who must choose from the various alternatives open to him. In such situations he needs moral norms to guide him in the process of giving preference to one of the competing values or disvalues. By divesting his normative theory of the preference principle, Knauer will certainly leave such a helpless fellow in a lurch.

In conclusion it is necessary to point out that in view of the pitfalls in Knauer's argumentation, his reinterpretation of the principle of double effect is hardly acceptable.

5.

FRANZ SCHOLZ' REINTERPRETATION OF THE PRINCIPLE OF DOUBLE EFFECT

Franz Scholz devotes space in two of his works (1) to reexamining the moral relevance of the direct/indirect distinction of the principle of double effect as it is traditionally applied to acts teleologically normed, which he describes as "Abwägungsprohibitiv" and to those deontologically appraised, which he refers to as "Naturprohibitiv" or "Wesensprohibitiv". The principle in its traditional formulation, he notes, rightly applies to acts teleologically assessed. Direct scandal, for instance, is always prohibited, indirect scandal is permissible for a proportionate reason (2).

Regarding the question whether the principle in its traditional understanding applies correctly to acts deontologically evaluated, Scholz expresses some sceptical reserve. He argues that, although the principle serves the catholic tradition the useful purpose of a restrictive interpretation of deontoligical norms (3), moralists are not thereby entitled to thinking that such acts can ever be indirectly intended. Thus opposed to the teaching of the handbooks of moral theology he argues that acts deontologically appraised, by their very nature, can only be directly intended. Accordingly, he reformulates the principle of double effect as it is applicable to such acts as follows: "Direct, yes, but only for a corresponding grave reason." (4)

One sees at first glance that Scholz, in this way, dissolves the principle of double effect simply into the fundamental principle of a teleological ethics. In this regard, he follows the footprints of Knauer. Nevertheless, he is of the opinion that in the presence of a proportionate reason one may also **directly** intend the evil effect of an act, while Knauer, in contrast, maintains that a proportionate reason makes the evil effect of an act into something indirectly intended. In the face of the striking similarity existing between their positions in as much as they transform the principle of double effect into a teleological rule, one immediately conjectures that this difference is more terminological in nature than substantial.

----

1 Franz Scholz, **Wege, Umwege und Auswege der Moraltheologie.** Ein Plädoyer für begründete Ausnahmen. München 1976; "Object und Umstände, Wesenswirkungen und Nebeneffekte," in: **Christlich glauben und handeln,** ed. Klaus Demmer and Bruno Schüller, Düsseldorf, Patmos 1977, pp. 243-260. This is the Festschrift in honour of Joseph Fuchs, S. 3.

2 ibid. pp. 257-258; **Wege, Umwege** ... pp. 81-82.

3 ibid. 40 ff.

4 ibid. pp. 126.

The argumentative strategies Scholz employs in getting at his conclusion are worth attending to. Since he uses different arguments in his different works, it will be more convenient to examine each of the works separately.

5.1. EXPOSITION OF THE ARGUMENTS IN WEGE; UMWEGE UND AUSWEGE ...

In his **Wege, Umwege und Auswege der Moraltheologie** Scholz deals with the problem of the direct/indirect distinction of the principle of double effect in a very extensive manner. Since dealing with all the issues he raised in this book is far beyond the scope of this work, efforts will be made to concentrate, as much as possible, only on the essentials of the arguments he employs here.

To demonstrate that the evil effects proceeding from acts deontologically appraised are always directly intended, Scholz tests the realizability of the conditions of the principle of double effect against some concrete applications of the principle. Among these are:

1) By removing the diseased uterus of a pregnant woman by means of a surgical procedure the death of the foetus, which is foreseen, occurs during the operation. The attack on the life of the embryo which results from this procedure is usually considered indirectly intended by Tradition.

2) A horse-rider, who takes to flight in order to save his life, foresees that he will trample a child to death who is lying across the path through which he is galloping to safety. Inspite of the foreseen causation of death he continues his escape. Usually some handbooks of moral theology describe the killing of the child as an unintended side-effect.

In examining the first example Scholz concedes that Tradition is right when it judges that the uterus of the woman may be rightly removed by a surgical operation, if the cancer threatens the life of the woman. Nevertheless, Tradition, according to him, makes a mistake in thinking that the death of the child in this case is only indirectly intended. Actually one cannot undertake the surgical operation without **directly** intending the death of the child, since the child's death and the restoration of the woman's health stand in a means-to-end relationship (5). Thus Tradition holds that such a case, which it terms indirect killing but which Scholz sees as direct killing, demands nothing more and nothing less than a proportionate reason for its moral justification.

In analysing the second example Scholz asserts that the persecuted man, seeing his life in danger, finds "riding away" on a horse as a means to saving his life. However, he maintains that as soon as

---

5 ibid. p. 97.

the child comes within view the means to safety becomes "gallopping away and thereby trampling a child." Just as in the preceeding example, he tries to deduce from this that the destruction of the child's life and the saving of the man's life stand in a lineal relationship of means-to-end (6).

In addition, like Suarez and Prümmer he refers to **Summa Theologica** I, II, q. 1, a. 3, ad. 3 and maintains that an act has only one essential effect. Should this essential effect be evil, the good will necessarily proceed from it and not side by side with it (7).

Having made these points he proceeds to showing that since the death of the foetus and the restoration of the woman's health in the first example as well as the death of the child and the saving of the horse-rider's life in the second example relate to each other as means-to-end, only a direct willing of the death of the child is possible in each case. By willing the end the necessary means to it is also necessarily willed. Arguing in this manner, he concludes that the condition of the principle requiring that only the good effect should be intended is also not concretely realizable (8).

Next he proceeds to showing that where both of the above conditions of the principle of double effect are not concretely realized, that requiring the act to be good or at least indifferent cannot be attained, either. To demonstrate this claim, he asserts that the basic act in the example is not "riding" but rather "Killing an innocent person while riding," an act which is in itself intrinsically (morally) evil (9).

Having tried to show that the above three conditions of the principle of double effect are not concretely operative he goes on to conclude that only the condition which demands a proportionate reason is functional. Thus the persecuted man, in choosing the course of his action, believes that the death of the child is a proportionate "price" to pay for saving his life.

5.1.1.   APPRECIATION OF SCHOLZ' ARGUMENTS

Scholz deserves much praise for his painstaking analysis of the principle of double effect and its application. He is right in declaring that the principle applies validly to acts teleologically normed. He is also correct in pointing out that the principle applied to acts deontologically normed serves tradition the useful purpose of a restrictive interpretation of deontological norms. In this way tradition pro-

----

6   ibid, pp. 84-85.

7   ibid. pp. 88 ff.

8   ibid. pp. 98 ff.

9   ibid. pp. 102-103.

fesses that it is no stranger to and lover of the headaches and heart-breaks of life and is able to side-tract the tragic situations which a strict observation of such norms would otherwise bring about.

In examining the arguments employed by Scholz in his **Wege, Umwege und Auswege der Moraltheologie**, it might be appropriate isolating that based on the **Summa Theologica** which states that an act, by its very nature, has only one essential effect. Since this argument has been extensively dealt with in examining the position held by Suarez, there is no use devoting more space to it again. What is then to be said of the other argument?

It is by no means easy to see how this reasoning is to be seen as logically conclusive. Apparently, for Scholz it is from the word go a foregone conclusion that Tradition argues correctly only when it reasons teleologically. He, thus, devotes himself solely and merely towards showing that it undercuts its deontological norms by applying the principle of double effect to them. In comparison to Tradition, some more logical consistency in reasoning is required and every deontological norm would be overcome as something left behind.

Scholz overlooks the fact that were the lack of logical consistency to be proved to Tradition, it could obviate it by revoking in all its forms as illegitimate the restrictive interpretation of deontological norms it has up till now practised by employing the principle of double effect.

In this regard one can simply recall that in the past some moral theologians believed that one could morally justify a direct abortion medically indicated to save the mother by arguing that it is killing an unjust aggressor in self-defence of the mother's life. These moralists were, no doubt, driven by a teleological reasoning. In reply to them the Holy Office (10) insisted that direct killing in a case of self defence cannot be seen as analogous to direct abortion. It is well-known that what resulted from this was not the general permission of a medically indicated direct abortion. Rather what proceeded from it was that one is bound to let mother and child die instead of saving the life of the mother through a directly intended killing of the child.

Apparently the Holy Office was so convinced of the validity of the deontological prohibition of killing that it did not hesistate in the least to refuse this restrictive interpretation in so far as the latter apparently aims at eliminating the former. Scholz may reckon with some degree of certainty that Tradition will clear up the inconsistency towards a teleological ethics which he wants to prove to it should he first and foremost convince it that the deontological norms propagated by it are not rightly grounded. It is remarkable to note that Scholz does not in the least take his step which is necessary in order to convince Tradition on this issue.

Now what is the position of the lack of consistency in the reasoning of traditional moral theology? Does Scholz succeed in proving this deficiency by a correct reasoning? By trying to prove this, he partial-

---

10 cf. John Cornery, **Abortion**, pp. 291 ff.

ly commits the error indicated above in as much as he analyzes the length and breath of examples which are in fact doubtful applications of the principle and which found no undisputable acceptance in Tradition. One could grant that Scholz correctly analyzed these examples by bringing their evil and good effects into the relationship of causing evil as a means to achieving an intended good and that notwithstanding push the whole issue aside with the remark: "abusus non tollit usum".

To put it shortly, Scholz, by insisting that the evil and good effects of acts deontologically normed relate to each other as means-to-an-end and so always directly willed should have logically concluded that Tradition is wrong in applying the principle of double effect to these acts and should consequently insist that Tradition should propound a deontological ethics as strict and unyielding as Kant's. Where Scholz does not want to take this stand, it is incumbent on him to show first that Tradition is wrong in holding deontological norms before melting the principle of double effect into a teleological rule, as he does.

Having made this point it is worthwhile to stress that Scholz' illustration of the direct/indirect distinction with the case of the man fleeing to safety on a horse who thereby crushes the head of a child lying accross the narrow path leaves much to be desired. It is an example from the "grey-zone" - a blurring borderline case which fails to project the character of an indirect intended act in a crystal clear manner. Scholz' readers would have been all more the wiser had he been able to sustain his claim that the evil and good effects of acts deontologically assessed have a means-to-end relationship by employing more vivid examples found in the hand-books like:

a) killing non-combatants and combatants with a bomb in just war;

b) taking a pill which at once produces contraceptive and curative effects;

c) taking an injection which has both lethal and pain relieving effects.

It is hard to conceive how these pairs of evil and good effects which proceed from their (per se) cause directly and immediately, as well as, independent from each other can be rightly considered as having a means-to-end relationship.

By employing the rather blurring example of the man fleeing to rescue on a horse to show that the condition of the principle of double effect requiring the good effect to follow from the act at least directly and immediately as the evil is not concretely realizable, Scholz reaches the conclusion that the conditions demanding that:

a) the act should not be evil in itself; and

b) only the good effect should be intended; are also concretely unrealizable. Since his example is an inadequate illustration of that condition of the principle and since there are many concrete examples that prove the contrary, Scholz' conclusion regarding the realizability of the other two conditions is untenable. This is because it is founded on a faulty premise.

129

In addition, it is instructive to note that Prümmer to whom Scholz recourses now and again in proving his claim (11), solves cases where a good can be achieved only when an (intrinsic) evil is caused by means of the principle of double effect as it is traditionally understood. He justifies, for instance, the killing of innocent noncombatants along with combatants in a just war; the taking of a drug by a pregnant woman, which has both curative and abortive effects and so on not by asserting that they are "direct but justifiable for a proportionate reason" as Scholz does. Rather he judges them "indirect" and permits them for a proportionate reason (12). Having in mind that Prümmer applies the principle of double to acts deontologically evaluated in a manner that agrees with traditional practice, one wonders whether Scholz has interpreted him correctly.

Last but not least Scholz claims that an act cannot "de facto" produce evil and good effects simultaneously also requires attention. It appears that Scholz assumes that Tradition speaks of an act which simultaneously produces good and evil effects only because it intends to classify the latter as unintended side-effect (Nebenwirkung) and in order to create for itself the possibility of interpreting the deontological norms restrictively. Thus, he criticizes, as it were, Tradition's ideology on this point. However, he fails to make a counter investigation in other areas of life to see whether this terminology is also employed in the sense Tradition uses it, that is to say, whether the evil effect which accompanies the intended good effect of an action is also described as "an unintended side-effect". This is indeed the case in the pharmaceutical description of the effects of drugs. Among other things the directives obtainable in the packets of drugs indicate the side-effects that could accompany the healing effects of the drug in question. "Side-effect", which has equivalent expressions in other languages (13), is not a word signifying nothing; it is a term designating some reality as is discernable from the information of the following Dictionaries:

1) A.S. Hornby (14), **Oxford Advanced Learners Dictionary**, side effect: secondary or indirect effect, e.g. an undesirable effect of a drug used for a specific purpose.

2) **Collins English Dictionary**, (15)
   side effect: 1. any unwanted nontherapeutic effect caused by a drug.

   2. any secondary effect, esp. an undesirable one.

----

11 F. Scholz, **Wege, Umwege** ... pp. 80, 81, 95.

12 D.M. Prümmer, **Manuale Theologiae Moralis**, vol. 2, Friburgi Herder 1955, no. 132, pp. 124-125.

13 For instance the Germans call it "Nebenwirkung". French men refer to it as 'Effet secondaire'.

14 A.S. Hornby, **Oxford Advanced Learners Dictionary**, Oxford 1980.

15 **Collins English Dictionary**, London & Glasgow 2 ed. 1980.

3) **Chamber's Twentieth Century Dictionary**, (16)
Side effect: A subsidiary effect: an effect, often undesirable, additional to the effect sought.

4) **The Random House Dictionary of English Language**, (17)
Side effect: An effect of a drug, chemical or other medicine that is additional to its intended effect especially an effect that is harmful or unpleasant.

It is scarcely to be imagined that the authors of the Dictionaries cited above are acquainted with the teaching of catholic tradition on the principle of double effect and are as a result influenced by it as they made the entry of the cited texts. At the same time they portray the vocabulary of this teaching in important points, from which one may infer that the use of this vocabulary for the description of an act with a double effect springs from the character of the act itself. At the same time this clarification of term may serve to clear up some misunderstanding of the word "side-effect". "Side-effect" does not mean "side issue" or "unimportant effect". It rather means the effect alongside or additional to the intended effect. Thus, when "side-effect" is used to refer to a "secondary effect", it is not to be taken as depicting something of secondary importance but rather as referring to the second of two things considered arithmetically.

5.2. EXPOSITION OF THE ARGUMENTS IN "OBJEKT UND UMSTÄNDE, WESENSWIRKUNGEN UND NEBENEFFEKTE."

The argument employed by Scholz in his article, "Objekt und Umstände, Wesenswirkungen und Nebeneffekte," are complicated and so call for more detailed exposition. In this work Scholz reappraises the traditional notions of object/circumstance and effectus per se/effectus per accidens. The object of an act, he notes, is traditionally described in a manner that permits the presentation of an evil effect as a side-effect. Within this model essential circumstances (quid and cur) which are integrated into the object in an act-description and whose role in determining the character of an act are decisive are merely deemed "accidents."

Furthermore, the essential effects proceeding from such objects are degraded to mere side-effects and so considered elegible candidates of indirect voluntariness. Scholz believes that it is a logical error to name essential circumstances "accidents." In addition, he asserts that classifying essential effects as side-effects is also a mistake.

----

16 A.M. Macdonald, **Chamber's Twentieth Century Dictionary**, London 1972.

17 Tess Stein, **The Random House Dictionary of English Language**, New York 1969.

He locates the source of the former error in the narrower notion of circumstance developed by St Thomas Aquinas. Thomas asserts that "circumstantia dicitur quasi extra substantiam actus existens, ita tamen, quod aliquando attingit eum" (S. Th., I, II, q. 7, a. 3). Later in the same passage he asserts that circumstances are "accidents."

Moreover, Scholz points out that Thomas teaches that circumstances are "accidents." In his view this doctrine is not logically reconcilable with Thomas' assertion that circumstances are "accidents." To his mind this error can be avoided if circumstances were not to be seen as "accidents" but as "variables." (18) This is because circumstances operate like variables in determining the character of an act; sometimes their role is of very little importance; at other times decisive.

Furthermore, Scholz tries to indicate that the variable nature of circumstance is important for the understanding of side-effects. Only circumstances that are not essential (circumstances) can produce side-effects. In such instances the production of side-effects indicate that more than one cause is at work.

A circumstance which is assimilated into the description of the object, namely, an essential circumstance does not produce a side-effect; it produces only an essential effect, which is identifiable with the "finis operis." In a case like this, Scholz says that only a cause is at work, and its natural effect is certain to follow. Since an essential effect cannot be rightly described as a side-effect, it cannot be the object of indirect voluntariness. Furthermore since the essential effect is identifiable with the "finis operis" (object) it is necessarily the subject of direct intention. For some manuals of moral theology define the object of an act as "that to which will primarily and per se according to its relation with the moral norm." (19)

To the basic question as to which circumstance in a given case must be counted as part of the object and which remains an accident, Scholz replies that this cannot be determined "a priori." The concrete situation is the test ground. Once this is established actions that are necessarily "direct" and those that are "indirect" are immediately evident.

To illustrate his thesis, Scholz draws some concrete examples from the manuals.

1. Christ heals a man with a whithered hand on a Sabbath day. This gives rise to pharisaic scandal (Mk 3, 1-6).

2. An unarmed person meets a deadly enemy intent on slaying him. The only way of saving his life is by fleeing on a horse through a narrow path occupied by a child or a blind or a cripple. He takes flight on his horse, foreseeing that he will kill an innocent person in the process. Traditional manuals justify the killing of an innocent

----

18 Franz Scholz, "Objekt und Umstände ..." p. 248.

19 cf. Arthurus Vermeersch: **Theologiae Moralis**, vol. 1 Parisiis 1933, p. 110.

person in this instance as accidental, or as an unintended side-effect.

3. Innocent persons are present in a fortress attacked by the enemy. Traditional manuals justify this action in which innocent persons are killed by asserting that only the death of the combatants is intended. The killing of the innocent is described as a foreseen but unintended side-effect.

Scholz inquires whether these examples portray side-effect which are objects of indirect intention. To the first he answers positively. He believes that in this case a true side effect is at hand. He, who seeks his objective by an "actio minus recta" does not cause the neighbour's sin. The operation of another is necessary for a true side-effect. Therefore the psychology of the will does not demand that the evil effect be willed either as a means or as a "conditio sine qua non."

As to the question whether the other examples are cases of in-direct intention, Scholz replies negatively. In the second example manuals describe the object of the act as "fleeing down the road on a horse." Scholz disagrees with this description as a preprogrammed object (20). Excluding the presence of the blind or the child from the range of the object stands opposed to reality. He maintains that the presence of the child or blind on the path is of such a momentous importance that it should be assimilated into the description of the ob-ject. Thus it is evident that this is an essential effect.

Therefore the escaper cannot claim that he only permitted the death of the innocent. The death in this case is the means by which he escapes. But the means, just as the end, can only be directly intended. A true side-effect is only conceivable, in the case describ-ed, if the victims threw themselves at the last moment into the path through which the rider is fleeing. In this case the rider can say he permits what he cannot prevent.

With regard to the third example, the attacker might say that he wishes only to kill combatants. But the single natural effect of the bombing is the destruction of combatants and non-combatants. His regrets at the death of non-combatants indicates only that their deaths are not intended "propter se sed propter aliud." Their death is a "conditio sine non" for the attainment of the good end. But he who is prepared under the call of the end to realize the "conditio sine qua non" acts exactly the same way as the one who chooses the appropriate means, namely, he who wills it directly.

Accordingly, in the two last examples Scholz does not believe that the deaths of the innocent are indirectly intended. He maintains that these effects, like all natural effects are directly intended. Since to his mind such essential evil effects can only be, directly intended, he thus moves for a new model: "direct, yes, but only for a pro-portionate grave reason."

---

20 Franz Scholz, "Objekt und Umstände ..." p. 254.

5.2.1. APPRECIATION OF THE ARGUMENTS

For the purpose of a deeper appreciation of some of the issues raised by Scholz, it may be worthwhile to recapitulate and reconstruct his argumentative strategy. His reasoning takes the following steps: Circumstances can not be rightly described as "accidents" because there are some circumstances that play a decisive role in determining the character of an act. Since essential circumstances determine the character of an act, they can not be said to produce side-effects but essential effects. Since an essential effect can not be deemed a side-effect, it can not be an object of indirect intention. Therefore, an essential effect is always directly willed.

Two points in this argument deserve closer attention:

a) Circumstances are not "accidents" but variables; and

b) essential circumstances produce only essential effects.

5.2.1.1. Circumstances are not accidents but variables

In his famous and widely read book, **Logic Matters**, Peter Thomas Geach alerts moralists against a very simple fact which is often glossed over in moral discussions when he remarks:

> "There is a reason why moral arguments often are incon-
> clusive and lead only to quarrels: namely, people may
> start a moral disputation when, as regards one of the key
> terms, they are not initially in agreement either on a
> class of instances to which it applies or on criteria for
> applying it ..." (21)

This cute observation is no less true when a term like "accident" is employed in moral reasoning. A word with a wide range of meaning, "accident" can be used differently in different contexts. In common parlance, for instance, the term refers to a change occurrence. It is used to describe a fall or a collision, with or without personal injuries. Its adjectival form, accidental, is frequently employed to refer to the aspect of a thing or event that is considered less important or superficial.

Ancient and medieval philosophers employed the term in logic in their discussion over the predicables (genus, specis, difference, property and accident) in another sense. They point out that when something is said of a subject it can either a) belong to the nature or essence of the subject and express its quiddity or b) pertain to the subject in some way other than its essence, that is to say, as an

----

21 Peter Thomas Geach, **Logic Matters**, Oxford Blackwell 1972, p. 3.

accident. In this latter case what is predicated of a subject may indicate something contingently associated with it. Here "accident" means the same as not essential to the concept of a substance, or simply, non-essential.

Evidently Scholz takes "accident" as employed by Thomas in S. Th., I, II, q. 7, a. 1 and by the manuals in the teaching on circumstances to mean the same as non-essential. Thus Scholz would argue that if there are circumstances which play a decisive role in determining the character of an act, it would be illogical to refer to circumstances as accidents (non-essentials). Put conversely, if every circumstance is an accident, then it cannot be right to talk of essential circumstances.

The logical implication of the point Scholz is making becomes more vivid when the propositions:

a) every circumstance is an accident

b) some circumstances are not accidents (non-essential)

c) some circumstances are accidents (non-essential) are placed on a "Quadratus Pselli"

Every circumstance is an accident.

No circumstance is an accident.

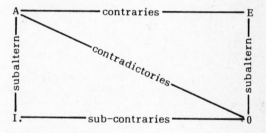

Some circumstances are accidents.

Some circumstances are not accidents.

In his argumentation Scholz pairs propositions A and 0 together and understands "accident" in each case as "non-essential" to the moral determination of the character of an action. Since the propositions relate to each other as contradictories, if 0 is true, then A is false. Thus since 0 is in fact true, A is necessarily false. Thus Scholz moves for the abandonment of proposition A.

It is true that in the teachings of St Thomas Aquinas and the manuals, propositions I and 0 are obtainable, if "accidents" were to be understood as non-essential to the moral determination of the character of an action. For while some circumstances are known as "circumstantiae speciem non mutantes" others are called "circumstantiae speciem mutantes." By asserting that circumstances are variables, Scholz pinpoints exactly at what Thomas and the manuals mean

135

here.

It is also true that a statement worded like proposition A is to be found in the writings of St Thomas and in the manuals. It is, nevertheless, another question whether interpreting "accident" in this context as that non-essential for the moral determination of an act, as Scholz does, is right. By making statement A, Thomas and the manuals employ "accident" as a logical predicate depicting something outside the substance of the action or object described.

Since Scholz' interpretation of Thomas use of "accident" is disputable, it might be worthwhile to let Thomas speak at length for himself. Remarking that man, in his linguistic habits, tends to transfer the names of more obvious things to those less obvious, Thomas proceeds to say:

> "... in like manner words that signify local movement are employed to designate all other movements, because bodies which are circumscribed by place, are best known to us. And hence it is that the word circumstance has passed from located things to human acts. Now in things located, that is said to surround something, which is outside it, but touches it, or is placed near it. Accordingly whatever conditions are outside the substance of an act, and yet in some way touch the human act, are called circumstances. Now that is outside a substance while it belongs to that thing, is called its accident. Wherefore the circumstances of human acts should be called their accident" (S. Th., I, II, q. 7, a. 1).

It is obvious from the context that the assertion: "circumstances are accidents" is metaphorical. Important in considering a metaphorical statement is that an interpreter grasps the "tertium comparationis". A metaphorical statement like the classroom example: "My love is a rose", like all metaphorical statements, is equivocal, because the "verbum translatum", rose, can signify beauty, passing-away or thorny. Thus the statement can mean:

a) My love is beautiful, or

b) My love is passing-away, or

c) My love is thorny.

Thus to get at the meaning the speaker or writer intends, an interpreter has to consult the context. He has to see from the context what aspect of the "verbum translatum" is being compared with the subject (verbum proprium). Similarly, to understand the meaning of Thomas' assertion, "circumstances are accidents" one has to consult its context.

Here Thomas draws some parallels. Just as things extrinsic to located things but which are close to them or which touch them are called circumstances, conditions to human acts but which pertain to them are, similarly, called circumstances. Furthermore, just as things extrinsic to a substance but which belong to it are called its "accidents", similarly elements extrinsic to a human act but pertain to it are called its accidents. In a word, Thomas employs the term "accident" as a logical predicate referring to elements related to a human act which are not included in the description of the act or the act-term employed.

By declaring that circumstances are accidents, Thomas does not make any reference to the role circumstances play in determining the character of an act. Seen in this way, the Angelic Doctor cannot be rightly said to be wallowing in a logical error when he says that circumstances are accidents and at the same time holds that certain circumstances (circumstantiae speciem mutantes) play a decisive role in determining the moral character of an act.

5.2.1.2. Essential circumstances produce only essential effects

In order to prove that the principle of double effect does not apply to acts deontologically normed, Scholz finds it necessary stressing that essential circumstances produce only essential effects; they do not produce side-effects. This claim offers him the point of departure for raising some objection against the traditional tendency of describing the object of human acts in a manner that allows them to be deemed indifferent to moral rightness or wrongness. The case in point is the so called indifferent objects or acts. A few concrete examples.

The object of the act of the man who jumps to death through the window from a five storey building in order to escape a more excruciating death by fire, is often presented in the manuals as "jumping out of the window". Similarly, the object of the act of a man, who, in striving to escape from a mortal enemy by horse, maims and kills cripples lying on the path through which he is riding is described as "fleeing down the path on a horse."

Although one may feel dissatisfied or even outraged at such descriptions of the object, no descriptive rule, linguistic or otherwise, makes such descriptions reproachable. This is because notions of objects as well as circumstances are highly indeterminate and elastic (22). The borderline separating the two shifts according to what elements of a human performance are chosen or delimited by the word standing for the object. One searches in vain in the dictionary for words that always stand for the object or circumstances. An element of action can be considered a circumstance in one act description, while in another it is deemed a part of the object.

Suppose a given human performance comprises features a, b, c, and d. If "a" and "b" are covered by the term depicting the object of the act, then "c" and "d" are circumstances. If in another description the term indicating the object of the act only incorporates "a" in its comprehension then "b", "c" and "d" count for circumstances.

If goaded by a feeling of revenge A willfully shoots B in a church, the object of A's could be described as murder, if one chooses to look at the event from the perspective of the fifth commandment. In this case, the fact that the event took place in the church

---

22   cf. I, II, q. 18, a. 10; q. 88, a. 5

is classified as a circumstance. If on the other hand, the event is considered from the view-point of the virtue or religion the object of the act will be termed sacrilege. In this case the fact than an innocent person is killed is deemed a circumstance (23).

Since the classification of the elements of an action into the categories of object and circumstance varies and since this classification depends largely, if not solely, on the perspective that is under consideration, it would not be right to insist, as Scholz does, that a particular element of an action like an essential circumstance must be incorporated in an object-description. Essential circumstances may determine the "finis operis" (object) of an action, if they are assimilated by the word standing for the object. But if they are excluded by this term, they do not determine the "finis operis".

It might be worthwhile to stress that the relevant ethical question in the case where a man maims or kills cripples in his flight to safety is not whether the description of the object of the act as "fleeing down the path" is right or wrong. This is a linguistic question. The question that interests a moralist in this case is: given the circumstances of trying to save his life from a mortal enemy and foreseeing the maiming or killing of cripples in the process, whether it is morally right or wrong to flee down the path. This is the question to which the principle of double effect addresses itself.

This is, as it were, a case of a double action. Viewed from one perspective it is a case of killing an innocent person. Viewed from another, it is a life-saving action. It is a case where a man seems obliged not to flee in order to avoid maiming and killing innocent persons and at the same time bound to take flight in order to save his life.

In conclusion it may be said that Scholz is right in altering the principle of double effect to "Direct, yes, but for a proportionate reason" in the sector of acts deontologically evaluated, if the causing of the evil (effect) in question here is seen as the causing of a non-moral disvalue. For a proportionate reason one may legitimately intend to cause a non-moral disvalue as an instrumental good (bonum utile). But to reach this conclusion by arguing that the acts deontologically evaluated are "ex definitione" not objects of indirect intention is hardly convincing.

---

23 cf. Benedictus H. Merkelbach, **Summa Theologiae Moralis**, vol. 1, Brugis 1959, pp. 242.

CONCLUSION

The principle of double effect was not meant by Tradition, to be applicable to every act which produces good and evil, it was designed to govern acts which are said to produce good and intrinsic (moral) evil simultaneously. Its formulation rests on the belief that some disvalue are 'per se' intrinsically (morally) evil. Thus this rule perdures or ceases to exist with the rightness or wrongness of this presupposition.

Since it is not disputable that the disvalues (scandal and the cooperation in the sin of the others) produced by acts teleologically normed are intrinsically (morally) evil, the principle endures in this respect. Since it is debatable that the disvalues produced by the acts deontologically appraised are intrinsically (morally) evil, the principle endures or vanishes to the extent the deontological norms are rightly or wrongly grounded. If tradition is right in grounding the deontological norms with the argument it employs, then the principle of double effect is morally relevant and has, as it were, an inalienable 'birth right' of existing with all its integral parts. If the principle has such a right of existence, does it require any reinterpretation?

Often many a moralist sets out to reinterprete the principle with the widely prevailing belief that Tradition makes a mistake in the formulation of the rule, particularly in its insistence that the evil effect should not be a means to the good intended. Propounding such a view is possible only to a moralist who, while peeping through teleological spectacles, sees the evils produced by the acts governed by the principle as non-moral. However, if Tradition, by employing a deontological argumentation, were to be right in considering the disvalues produced by these acts as intrinsically (morally) evil, no moralists worth the name would object to the principle's insisting that an intrinsical (moral) evil should not be a means to achieving the intended good. If these disvalues were really intrinsically (morally) evil, nobody would waste time trying to reinterprete the principle of double effect, just as nobody finds it necessary to reinterprete the rule as it applies to the teleological norms.

It is evident that the question regarding whether the principle of double effect is right or wrong in insisting that the evil effect should not be a means to the intended good depends on the rightness or wrongness of the more fundamental question of regarding these evils as intrinsic (moral) evils on deontological grounds. This is a fundamental question whose answer naturally rests on whether Tradition is right or wrong in grounding these acts deontologically. A moralist who fails to attend to this question while dealing with the problems of the principle of double effect entirely misses the point. Overlooking the crux of a moral question in this manner only leads to an endless and inconclusive discussion.

If Tradition is to be proved wrong in its grounding of the deontological norms, these norms are 'ipso facto' to be replaced by the teleological. Since the teleological norms do not need to be restrictively interpreted, it follows that the principle of double effect is redundant. If the existence of the rule is superflous its reinterpretation serves no use.

It is to be inferred from the foregoing that whether Tradition is wrong or right in its grounding of the deontological norms, the principle of double effect requires no reinterpretation.

ABBREVIATIONS

AAS	Acta apostolicae sedis
BAC	Biblioteca de autores cristianos
disp.	disputatio
dub.	dubium
EpThL	Ephemerides Theologia Lovanienses
G.S.	Gaudium et spes
NRTh	Nouvelle Revue Théologique
Periodica	Periodica de re morali, canonica, liturgica
PL	Patrologia Latina
RevSR	Revue des Sciences Religieuses
S.Th.	Summa Theologica S. Thomae Aquinatis
t.	tomus
ThGl	Theologie und Glaube
ThPh	Theologie und Philosophie
ThPQ	Theologisch-praktische Quartalsschrift
ThSt	Theological Studies
tr.	tractus
TThZ	Trierer theologische Zeitschrift

BIBLIOGRAPHY

I. WORKS DEALING WITH THE PRINCIPLE OF DOUBLE EFFECT

AERTNYS, J. : **Theologia Moralis,** secundum doctrinam S. Alphonsi Mariae de Ligorio doctoris ecclesiae, 2 vols., Paderbornae Ferdinard Schönigh 1901.

ALONSO, V.M. : **El principio del doble effecto en los comentadores de Sancto Tomas de Aquino,** Rome 1937.

ATTARD, M. : **Compromise in Morality,** Rome 1976.

BECANUS, M. : **De fide Spe et caritate,** Lugduni 1626.

BENDER, L. : "Occisio directa et indirecta", Ang. 28 (1951) 224-253.

BILLUART, C.R. : **Summa S. Thomae,** 9 vols., Lelouzey Paris n. d.

BLANDINO, G. : "Il principio fondamentale dell'etica", in: Rassegna di telogia, Suppl. n. 5 (1972) 104-108.

BÖCKLE, F. : **Fundamentalmoral,** München Kösel-Verlag 1977.

BOUSCAREN, T.L. : **Ethics of Ectopic Operations,** Milwaucee Bruce Pub. co. 1944.

CAHILL, L.S. : "Moral Methodology, A. case study", Chicago Studies 19 (1980) 171-87.

CAPONE, D. : "Il principio dell'azione con duplice effetto", in: **Medicina e Morale I.** Edizione Orizzonte Medico, 1968, 52-69.

CATHREIN, V. : **De Bonitate et Malitia Actuum Humanorum,** Louvain Museum Lessianum 1926.

–   **Moralphilosophie,** 2 vols. Freiburg im Breisgau Herder 1899. "Quo sensu secundum 5. Thomam ratio sit regula bonitatis voluntatis", Gregorianum, 12 (1931) 447-465.

CONWAY, W. : "The Act of Two Effects", in: Irish Theological Quarterly. 18 (1951) 125-137.

CORNEROTTE, L. : "Loi morale, valeurs humaines et situations de conflict", in: NRTh, 100 (1978) 502-532.

CURRAN, C./   Readings in **Moral Theology No. 1.** Moral Norms
MC CORMICK, R. : and Catholic Tradition, New York Paulist Press
eds.   1979.

CURRAN, C. : "Der Utilitarianismus und die heutige Moraltheologie – Stand der Diskussion", in: Concilium 12 (1976) 671-681.

–   Ongoing Revision in **Moral Theology,** Notre Dame 1965.

DE LIGORIO, A. : **Medulla Theologica Moralis R.P. Hermanni Busebaum societatis Jesu Theologi cum Adnotationibus,** (Nicapolii 1748)

–   **Theologia Moralis,** ed. Lonardus Gaude, Rome 1905.

DE LUGO, J. : Disputationes Scholasticae et morales, vol VI. De justi-
tiae et iure, Paris 1869.

DE VALENTIA, G. : Commentatorium Theologicorum, Benetiis 1605.

DE VITORIA, F. : Commentarios a la secunda secundae de Santa Tomas,
Salamanca 1934.

DE VIO CAJETAN, T. : Commentaria in Summan Theologicam S. Thomae
Aquinatis, Romae 1882.

DI IANNI, A. : "The Direct/Indirect Distinction in Morals" in: Thomist,
41 (1977) 350-380.

Directive 30 of the Ethical and Religious Directive for Catholic
Health Facities (Nov. 1971).

DINGJAN, F. : "Die Beschränktheit jedes sittlichen Handelns – Die
Rolle der Epikie und Diskretion", in: ThGl, 63 (1973) 288-308.

FOOT, P. : "The Problem of Abortion and the Doctrine of the Double
Effect", in: Oxford Review 5 (1976) 5-15.

FUCHS, J. : "Der Absolutheitscharakter sittlicher Handlungsnormen",
in: Testimonium Veritati – Philosophisch – theologische Studien
zu kirchlichen Fragen der Gegenwart (Frankfurt 1971) 211-240.

GEMELLI, A. : "De L'avortement indirect", in: NRTh 60 (1933) 500-527
and 577-599.

–   "Encore L'avorte indirect, Réponse an T.R.P. Vermeersch s.
j.", in: NRTh 60 (1933) 687-693.

GENICOT, E./ Institutiones Theologiae Moralis, 2 vols., Dewit Brussels
SALSMANS :   2 1927.

GHOOS, J. : "L'acte à double effet, Etude de Théologie positive", in:
EpThL 27 (1951) 30-52.

GINTERS, R. : Werte und Normen. Einführung in die Philosophische
und Theologische Ethik, Düsseldorf 1982.

GRISEZ, G. : Abortion: the Myths, the Realities and the Arguments,
New York – Cleveland 1970.

GURY, T.P. : Compendium theologiae moralis auctum et accomodatum a
H. Dumus, vol. I, Lyon Briday 2 1875.

HÄRING, B. : Das Gesetz Christi, 3 vols., Freiburg im Breisgau 1961.

HART, H.L.A. : "Intention and Punishment", in: ibid, Punishment and
Responsibility Essays in the Philosophy of Law, Oxford 2 1970.

HENDRIKS, N. : Le moyen mauvais pour obtenir une fin bonne. Essai
sur la troisième condition du principe de L'acte à double
effet, Roma Herder 1981.

HORGAN, E., ed. : Humanae Vitae and the Bishops. The Encyclical and
the Statements of the National Hierachies, Ireland 1972.

HÖRMANN, K. : "Die Bedeutung der konkreten Wirklichkeit für das sitt-
liche Tun nach Thomas von Aquin", in: ThPQ 123 (1975) 125-
128.

        –   An Introduction to Moral Theology, London 1961.

HUGHES, G.J. : "Killing and Letting Die", in: Month 236 (1975) 42-45.

HÜRTH, F. : Theologia Moralis, Romae Universitas Gregoriana 1948.

JANSSENS, L. : "Ontic Evil and Moral Evil", in: Louvain Studies 5 (1972) 115-156.

KELLY, G. : Medico - Moral Problems, St. Louis 1949.

KISELSTEIN, G. : "La causalité accidentelle en théologia moralia", in: EpThL 3 (1926) 493-502.

KNAUER, P. : "La détermination du bien et du mal moral par le principe du double effet", NRTh 87 (1965) 356-376.

        –   "The Hermeneutic Function of the Principle of Double Effect", Natural Law Forum 12 (1967) 132-162.

        –   "Das rechtverstandene Prinzip von der Doppelwirkung als Grundnorm jeder Gewissensentscheidung", in: ThGL 57 (1967) 107-133.

        –   "Überlegung zur moraltheologischen Prinzipienlehre der Enzyklika 'Humanae Vitae'", in: ThPh 45 (1970) 60-74.

        –   Der Glaube kommt vom Hören - Ökumenische Fundamentaltheologie, Graz - Wien - Köln 1978.

        –   "Fundamentalethik - Theologische als deontologische Normenbegründung", in: ThPh 55 (1980) 321-360.

KRAMER, H.G. : The Indirect Voluntary or Voluntarium in Causa, Washington 1935 (STD Dissertation Catholic University of America).

LAYMANN, P. : Theologia Moralis, Monachii Heinrich 1626.

LEHMKUHL, A. : Theologia Moralis, Freiburg 1914.

LEROUX, E. : "La causa à double effet", in: Revue ecclésiatisque de Liege, 19 (1928) 257-267.

LESSIUS, L. : De justitia et jure, Mediolani 1613.

LYNCH, J. : "Notes on Moral Theology", in: ThSt, 17 (1956) 169-170.

MANGAN, J. : "An Historical Analysis of the Principle of Double Effect", in: ThSt 10 (1949) 41-61.

MAUSBACH, J./ Katholische Moraltheologie, vols. 1 and 2 Münster 1954.
ERMECKE, G. :

MERKELBACH, B.H. : Summa Theologia Moralis ad mentem D. Thomae et ad normam iuris novi, vols. 1 and 2, Burgis Belgia 1956.

MC CORMICK, R. : "Das Prinzip der Doppelwirkung einer Handlung", in: Concilium, 12 (1976) 662-670.

        –   Doing Evil to Achieve Good. Moral choice in conflict situations, Chicago 1978.

        –   Notes on Moral Theology 1965 Through 1980, Washington D.C. 1981.

MEDINA, B. : **Exposito in Primam Secundam Angelici Doctoris,** Venice 1590.

MEUNIER, A. : "A propos de la cause à double effet", in: Revue ecclésiastique de Liege 34 (1975) 85-100.

MOLINA, L. : **De justitia et jure,** Monguntiae 1659.

MOLINSKI, W. : "Darf und Soll ich Ärgernis geben?" in: Orientierung 33 (1969) 219-222.

MURTAGH, J. : **Intrinsic Evil,** Roma 1973 (A doctorate dissertation submitted to Pontificia Universitas Gregorianum Rome).

NICHOLSON, S.T. : "Abortion and the Roman Catholic Church", in: JRE Studies in Religions Ethics/University of Tenessee 1978.

NOLDIN, H. : Über die Mitwirkung zur Sünde des Nebenmenschen", in: **Zeitschrift für Katholische Theologie,** 3 (1879) 494-526.

NOLDIN, H./ **Summa Theologiae Moralis** iuxta codicem iuris canonici, SCHMITT, A. : Rome vol. I 20 1929, vol. 2, 20 1939.

PALAZZINI, I. : "Principium duplicis effectus", in: Dictionarium Morale et Canonicum III, Roma Officium Libri Catholici 1966, pp. 781-782.

PESCHKE, C.H. : **Christian Ethics,** Alcester and Dublin C. Goodliffe Neale, vol. 1 1972, vol. 2 1978.

PRÜMMER, D.M. : **Manuale Theologiae Moralis** secundum principia S. Thomae Aquinatis vol. 1 and 2, Freiburg, Herder 1955.

–   "Medizinische Eingriffe in das keimende Leben betrachtet vom Standpunkt der Katholischen Moral", in: Linzer Quartalsschrift, 74 (1921) 565-570.

RAMSEY, P. : **War and the Christian Conscience** Durhan North Carolina Duke University Press 1961.

RANWEZ, E. : "De voluntario in causa", in: collationes Namurcenses 2 (1928) 21-27.

REGATILLO, E.F./ **Theologiae Moralis Summa** iuxta constitutionem Apos-
ZALBA, M. : toliciam" Deus scientiarum Dominus", Matriti Biblioteca de Autores Cristianos Tomus I 1952, Tomus II 1953.

ROBERT, C. : "La situation de "conflit" un thème dangereux de la théologie morale d'aujourd' hui, in: RecSR 44 (1970) 194-197.

ROHLING, A. : **Medulla theologiae moralis,** St. Louis 1875.

ROSSI, L. : Come si formula il principio del duplice effetto, in: Rivista del Clero italiano 42 (1961), 278-283.

–   "Diretto" e "indiretto" in teologia morale, in: Rivista di Teologia morale 3 (1971), 37-65.

–   Il limite del principio del duplice effetto in: Rivista di Teologia morale 4 (1972), 11-37.

–   Duplice effetto (principio del), in: Dizionario enciclopedico di teologia morale Roma, Edizion Paoline 1973 2, 272-287.

-      Il principio del "voluntario in causa", in: La Scuola Cattolica
       93 (1965), 331-352.

ROY, R. : "La coopération selon saint Alphonse de Liguori", in: Studia Moralia 6 (1968), 415-421.

SALMANTICENSES : **Cursus Theologicus**, 20 vols., Parisiis Bruxellis 1877.

-      **Cursus Theologiae Moralis**, 3 vols., Pezzana Paris 1714.

SANCHEZ, T. : **De sancto matrimonii sacramento**, Venetiis 1712.

-      Opus morale in Praecepta Dei, 2 vols., Monte Parmae 1723.

SCHILLING, O. : **Grundriss der Moraltheologie**, Freiburg Herder 2 1949.

SCHOLZ, F. : "Grundfragen der Moraltheologie in neuer Sicht", in: ThGL 21 (1978) 152-160.

-      "Objekt und Umstände Wesenswirkung und Nebeneffekte" in: Klaus Demmer/Bruno Schüller eds., **Christlich glauben und handeln**, Düsseldorf Patmos 1977.

-      **Wege, Umwege und Auswege der Moralethologie** – Ein Plädoyer für begründete Ausnahmen, München 1976.

SCHÜLLER, B. : "Direkte / indirekte Tötung", in: ThPh 47 (1972), 341-353.

-      "Neuere Beiträge zum Thema Begründung sittlicher Normen", in: Theologische Berichte, vol. 4, Zürich – Einsiedeln – Köln 1974, pp. 109-181.

-      "The Double Effect in Catholic Thought: a Reevaluation", in: Richard Mc Cormick/Paul Ramsey, eds., **Doing Evil to Achieve Good**, Chicago 1978, pp. 168-192.

-      **Die Begründung sittlicher Urteile.** Typen ethischer Argumentation in der Moraltheologie, Düsseldorf 2 1980.

SELLING, J.A. : "The Problem of Reinterpreting the Principle of Double Effect", in: Louvain Studies 8 (1981), 47-62.

SLEUMER, A. : **Die Mitwirkung zur Sünde des Nächsten**, Bonn 1907.

SUAREZ, F. : **Opera Omnia**, 28 vols., Carolus Berton ed., Parisiis 1856.

SYLVIUS, F. : **Commentarium in Summam Theologicam**, 4 vols., Belleoniana Venice 1726.

VAN DER MARCK, W. : **Love and Fertility.** Contemporary Questions about Birth Regulation, trans. C.A.L. Jarot, New York 1965.

-      **Toward a Christian Ethic.** Renewal in Moral Theology, trans. Denis J. Barrett, New York Newman Press 1967.

VAN DER POEL, C. : "The Principle of Double Effect", in: Charles Curran ed., **Absolutes in Moral Theology?** Washington Corpus Books 1968.

VASQUEZ, G. : **Opuscula Morali**, Lugduni 1620.

VERMEERSCH, A. : "De causalitate per se per accidens", in: Periodica, XXI (1932), 101*-116*.

\-   Avortement direct ou indirect. Response au T. R. P. Gemell o.
f. m.", in: NRTh 60 (1933), 600-620.

\-   **Theologiae Moralis Principia**, vols. 1 and 2, Romae 3 1945.

WEBER, H. : "Der Kompromiß in der Moral – Zu seiner theologischen
Bestimmung und Bewertung", in: TThZ 8 (1977), 99-118.

WIGGERS, J. : **De jure et justitia**, Louvanii 1651.

ZALBA, M. : **Theologiae Moralis Compendium**, I (BAC 175) 1958.

II.   WORKS DEALING WITH ISSUES RELATED TO THE PRINCIPLE OF DOUBLE EFFECT

ARISTOTLE : **Nicomachean Ethics**, trans. H. Rackham, London Harvard
Uni. Press 2 1934.

AQUINAS, T. : **Opera Omnia**, ed. Leonis XIII, 15 vols., S. c. Prop.
Fide Rome 1882 1930, Vivès ed., 32 vols., Paris 1880.

AUGUSTINE : Contra Mendacium in: P. L., 40, 537.

BENDER, L. : "Consulere minus malum", in: EpThL, 8 (1931), 592-614.

\-   "Ex duobus malis minus est eligendum?" in Periodica de re
morali canonica, Liturgica, 40 (1951), 256-264.

BROAD, C.D. : **Five Types of Ethical Theories**, London 11 1979.

BRUNEC, M. : "Mendacium – Intrinsice malum – sed absolute" in: Sales-
ianum 2 (1964), 608-683.

CHIRICO, P. : "Tension, Morality and Birth Control", in: ThSt, 28
(1967), 258-285.

CLOSKEY, N.J. : **Meta – Ethics and Normative Ethics**, The Hague 1969.

CONNERY, J. :   **Abortion:** The Development of the Roman Catholic perspective, Loyola Uni Press 1977.

\-   "Morality of Consequences: a critical appraisal", in: ThSt,
34 (1973), 396-414.

\-   "Notes on Moral Theology", in: ThSt 17 (1956), 559-561.

CROTTI, N. : "Conscience and Conflict", in: ThSt 32 (1971), 208-232.

CURRAN, C. : **Christian Morality**, London 1969.

D'ARCY, E. : **Human Acts**, Oxford Clarendon Press. 1969.

DEMMER, K. : "Entscheidung und Kompromiss", in: Gregorianum 53/2
(1972), 325-351.

DONNELL, T.J.O. : **Morals in Medicine**, Westminster Md. Newman Press
1962.

FLETCHER, J : **Morals and Medicine**, Boston Beacon Press Edition 1960.

\-   **Situation Ethics**, London SCM Press Ltd. 1966.

FORD, J. : "Notes on Moral Theology" in: ThSt, 16 (1955), 383 ff.

FRANKENA, W. : **Ethics**, New York 1963.

FUCHS, J. : Natural Law - A Theological Investigation, New York 1965.

HAMEL, E. : "Conferentiae Episcopales et Encyclica Humanae Vitae", Periodica 58 (1968), 243-49.

HANNIGAN, E.T. : "Is it ever lawful to advise the lesser of two evils?" in: Gregorianum 30 (1949), 104-129.

HARE, R.M. : The Language of Morals, New York 1982.

HART, H.L.A./ Causation in Law, Oxford Clarendon Press 1959.
HONORÉ, A.M. :

HARTMANN, N. : Ethik, Berlin 1962.

HEINRICH, F. ed. : Naturgesetz und christliche Ethik zur wissenschaftlichen Diskussion nach Humanae Vitae, München 1970.

HÖRMANN, H. : Die Prägung des sittlichen Wollens durch das Objekt nach Thomas von Aquin, in: Böckle/Groner eds., Moral zwischen Anspruch und Verantwortung, Düsseldorf 1964.

HURLEY, D. : "A New Moral Principle - when Right and Duty Clash", in: Furrow, 17 (1966), 614-622.

-       "In Defence of the Principle of Overriding Right", in: ThSt, 29 (1968), 301-309.

JANSSENS, L. : "Norms and Priorities in a Love Ethics", in: Louvain Studies 6 (1977), 207-238.

KELLY, G. : Pope Pius XII and the Principle of Totality in: ThSt 16 (1955), 373-396.

KERN, A. : Die Lüge, Graz 1930.

LINDWORSKY, J. : "Das Problem der Lüge bei Katholischen Ethikern und Moralisten", in: Otto Lipmann/Paul Plaut, eds., Die Lüge, Leipzig 1927.

LYONS, D. : Form and Limits of Utilitarianism, Oxford 1970.

MÜLLER, G. : Die Wahrhaftigkeitspflicht und die Lüge, Freiburg 1962.

NOLAN, M. : The Principle of Totality in the writings of Pope Pius XII, Rome Universitas Gregoriana 1963.

NOONAN, J. : Contraception: A history of its treatment by the Catholic Theologians and Canonists, Cambridge Harvard Univ. Press. 1970.

PAULSEN, F. : System der Ethik, Berlin 10 1913.

PAUL VI : Humanae Vitae, London C. T. S. 1968.

PINCKAERS, S. : "Le rôle de la fin dans L'action morale selon saint Thomas", in: Revue des science Philosophique et Theologiques 45 (1961), 393-421.

PLATO : Last days of Socrates, trans. Hugh Tredennick New York Penguin Books 1969.

REGAN, A. : "The Basic Morality of Organic Transplants between living Humans", in: Studia Moralia 3 (1965), 320-361.

REGAN, G.M. : "Natural Law in the Church Today", in: Catholic Lawyer 13 (1967), 21-41.

RUSSEL, T.L. : "Contraception and the Natural Law", Heythrop Journal 10 (1969), 121-134.

SCHÜLLER, B. : **Gesetz und Freiheit**. Eine moraltheologische Untersuchung, Düsseldorf 1966.

VERMEERSCH, A. : "De mendacio et necessitatibus commercii humani", Gregorianum 1 (1920), 11-40, 425-475.

WITTMANN, M. : "Stellung und Bedeutung des voluntarium in der Ethik des hl. Thomas von Aquin", in: Festg. C. Baeumker, Münster 1923.

III. OTHER CITED WORKS

–   **Acta Apostolicae Sedis.** Commentarium Officiale, vols. 1-74, Romae 1909-892.

BROWN, R.E. ed. : **The Jerome Biblical Commentary**, New York Engelwood Cliffs 1974.

EDWARDS, P. ed. : **The Encyclopedia of Philosophy**, 8 vols., London 2 1972.

FLANNERY, A. ed. : **Vatican II.** The conciliar and Post conciliar documents, Dublin 1975.

GEACH, P.T. : **Logic Matters**, Oxford Blackwell 1972.

HÖRMANN, K. : **Lexikon der christlichen Moral**, Wien Tyrolia-Verlag 2 1976.

JONES, A. ed. : **The Jerusalem Bible.** London 1966.

MACDONALD, A. M. : **Chamber's Twentieth Century Dictionary**, London 1972.

OFFIONG, M. : Unpublished Manuscripts on "Desacralization of Creation", Enugu Nigeria 1976.

PERRY, R.B. : **General Theory of Value**, Cambridge 1967.

RASHDALL, H. : **The Theory of Good and Evil**, London 2 1924.

STEIN, J. ed. : **The Random House Dictionary of English Language**, New York 1969.

WITTGENSTEIN, L. : **Philosophical Investigations**, tr. G.E.M. Anscombe, Basil Blackwell Oxford 1953.